M000198486

FACING GOD

FACING GOD

*Unlocking His Truth and Mercy
Through the Life of Job*

DAPHNE DELAY

Unless otherwise indicated, all Scripture quotations from the book of Job are taken from The New Living Translation, copyright © 1996 by Tyndale Charitable Trust. All rights reserved.

Scripture quotations marked NKJV are taken from the *New King James Version*. Copyright © 1979, 1980, 1982, Thomas Nelson, Inc.

Scripture quotations marked GW are taken from *God's Word*®, Copyright© 1995 God's Word to the Nations. Used by permission of Baker Publishing Group.

Scripture quotations marked MSG are taken from *The Message: New Testament with Psalms and Proverbs* copyright ©1993, 1994, 1995 by Eugene H. Peterson, published by NavPress, P.O. Box 35001, Colorado Springs, Colorado 80935. Used by permission.

Scripture quotations marked AMP are taken from *The Amplified Bible. Old Testament* copyright © 1965, 1987 by Zondervan Corporation, Grand Rapids, Michigan. *New Testament* copyright © 1954, 1958, 1987 by The Lockman Foundation, La Habra, California. Used by permission.

Scripture quotations marked TLB are from The Living Bible copyright ©1971 by Tyndale House Foundation. Used by permission of Tyndale House Publishers Inc., Carol Stream, Illinois 60188. All rights reserved. The Living Bible, TLB, and The Living Bible logo are registered trademarks of Tyndale House Publishers.

11 10 9 8 7 6 5 4 3 2 1   16 17 18 19

Facing God: Unlocking His Truth and Mercy Through the Life of Job

Copyright© 2016 by Daphne Delay

ISBN: 978-1-68031-096-2

Published by Harrison House Publishers

P.O. Box 35035

Tulsa, Oklahoma 74153

www.harrisonhouse.com

Printed in the United States of America.

All rights reserved under International Copyright Law. Contents and/or cover may not be reproduced in whole or in part without the expressed written consent of the Publisher.

Table of Contents

Preface

Emotions are high, and you could cut the tension with a knife. Job and his friends are deadlocked. What else could be said? Job's three friends don't know how to respond, so they fall silent. Job isn't budging or admitting one ounce of guilt. It seems to the others Job thinks he's pretty perfect and God is the one who is wrong. But a fifth man is standing by—Elihu is his name. He's been calm and quiet, but now his anger is kindled. In that moment, I stood in awe of what God was doing with the simple message of righteousness. The Holy Spirit whispered to me, "Write it down, and I'll put it in the hands of people you'll never meet."

Elihu is mad at Job. Really mad. Elihu can't believe the way Job has justified himself, even to the point of making himself out to be better than God. Elihu is also mad at Job's friends because they haven't come up with an answer to prove Job wrong. Until this deadlock, Elihu has said nothing. He is the youngest one, and it would be disrespectful, but he can't let it end like this. He has to say something.

Wide-eyed with shock, Elihu asks, "Really Job? Do you really want to say you are more righteous than God?" Elihu doesn't claim to know it all, but he is very clear in what he does believe about God: If it's a choice between you and God, Job, "I will ascribe righteousness to my Maker" (Job 36:3b, NKJV).

"Do you think it is right for you to claim, 'I am righteous before God'? For you also ask, 'What's in it for me? What's the use of living a righteous life?'" (Job 35:2–3). Elihu knows righteousness has always been God's to give, not man's to earn—as if God could owe a man anything. And as Elihu declares God's awesomeness to the four men, he is suddenly interrupted. "Then the Lord answered Job from the whirlwind: 'Who is this that questions my wisdom with such ignorant words?'" (Job 38:1–2).

The Bible is clear. God is addressing Job here, not Elihu. Elihu is right in confronting Job about thinking he is more righteous than God. But wait—isn't Job the same man God called "blameless"? What happened? Is it possible what God meant and what man has interpreted for centuries are two different things?

People have often claimed, "God said Job didn't sin, so he couldn't have been wrong." This isn't true. What the Bible actually says is, "In all of this, Job did not sin by blaming God" (Job 1:22), and "In all this Job did not sin with his lips" (Job 2:10b, NKJV). These are very clear descriptions of how Job didn't sin, but they are just as clear in how he slipped. People sin every day and never blame God for their actions. And the most dangerous of all sins are those of the heart, the sins that never cross our lips but build up under the surface just waiting for an opportunity to explode.

This is the story of the man who challenged God—the man God originally called blameless. But was he?

Are any of us?

CHAPTER ONE

What About...?

You may have picked up this book because you, like many before you, have asked the question, "What about Job?" But before we answer that question, we need to answer two other questions, namely "What about God?" and "What about human nature?"

As we study Job's life, we are also going to look closely at God and His character, for this is woven into the whole story.

To better understand things from God's perspective, however, perhaps we should begin by looking at our own frame of mind . For example, it would be wise to consider the scripture, "Who can say, 'I have made my heart clean, I am pure from my sin'?" (Proverbs 20:9, NKJV).

In our world, lives are built on a person's work or lack thereof. Children are taught from an early age to work hard in school, work hard to get a good job, work hard to keep the good job, and so on. In fact, to "work hard" and "do good" is nothing new—especially in the church. But in working hard, we find that two ditches line the road of life. One ditch is a frame of mind that keeps people under guilt and condemnation their entire lives—always feeling like they've fallen short somehow. People who think like this never fully realize what it means to have God's approval. It is the ditch of unworthiness.

The other ditch is the idea that "I have made my heart clean, I am pure from my sin." It begins as an attitude of the heart, nothing someone would claim aloud. But those who have slipped into this ditch only see the outside. They are unaware how much God cares about the issues of their hearts. It is the scary ditch of *self-righteousness.*

Both frames of mind creep in little by little. Like the 1/16 inch mark on a ruler, the error that has turned their feet off the path is almost too small to notice at first, but without correction, the distance from truth grows exponentially as they continue in that direction.

Dangerous Mindset

This book is about the error of self-righteousness and the ways in which it blinds good people who love God and want to serve Him with wholeheartedness, but are unaware that part of their heart has been overtaken. But to better understand this dangerous mindset, we need to first understand grace. Grace is defined as God's divine, unmerited favor available to the sinner for salvation and to the redeemed for victorious living.[1] The keyword here is *available*. Salvation is available to everyone. It had been offered to me my entire life, but I didn't accept God's grace and salvation until I was 21 years old. I later discovered that His grace was also available to me as a Christian, to help me grow and mature. But I didn't readily accept it then either. My entire life had been built on how good I could do on my own, so I naturally took that same mentality into my walk with God. I didn't understand this part of grace. I had been taught to be independent—that rewards were based on how good we do and how hard we work. Unfortunately, it is this works-based faith that fosters the hidden attitude of self-righteousness.

Working hard and doing good is actually a prevalent mind-set in the world (and should be), but it was born in the church. In Deuteronomy 6:25, Moses stood up before God's people and said, "It will be righteousness for us, if we are careful to observe all these commandments before the LORD our God, as He has commanded us" (NKJV). The righteousness Moses spoke of was right-standing (or approval) before God. In other words, Moses explained the only way to have God's favor and approval was to carefully observe (comply, follow, keep, and perform) all of His commandments.

Centuries later, this mentality still has Christians in a rut of religious duty, although this was never God's intention nor the people's aim. But when Moses said it, God's people followed the instruction to a tee. "For we will be counted righteous when we obey all the commands the LORD our God has given us" (Deuteronomy 6:25).

Impossible!

It's certainly understandable why the Israelites wanted God's approval. Who doesn't? And righteousness, by the purest definition, describes our ability to stand before God without guilt or inferiority as if we had never sinned. So you can see why "self" isn't part of the equation. But herein lies the first problem: According to Galatians 3:12, if you wish to find life by obeying the law (in other words: achieving it through human effort), then you must obey all of its commands in order to be made right with God. This is why the people were frustrated. They found it impossible to obey all of the Mosaic law, all of the time. Their failure was labeled as disobedience, which was labeled as sin—both of which disqualified them from God's promises.

The second problem they encountered is that we are human and, by nature, prone to sin. It's in our DNA. "When Adam sinned, sin entered the world. Adam's sin brought death, so death spread to everyone, for everyone sinned" (Romans 5:12). It just isn't possible for people to obey all of God's commands all of the time because every person has an inherited sin nature that causes them to miss the mark. And that's what sin means: to miss the mark. In this case, the "mark" was God's requirements. To miss that target in any way equaled sin.

And this brings us to the third problem: Because it's not humanly possible to obey all the law all of the time, many sensitive souls will naturally feel they can never be right with God.

The Process

The Bible says God fashioned our hearts individually, so He understands everything we do (Psalm 33:15). But He sees and knows things we cannot. He is the beginning and the end. Sometimes we get stuck because we try to understand God and His reasons for doing things based on our perspective and not His. God knew His people in advance. He knew full obedience to the law would be impossible. So He designed a process to help people. In Leviticus 17:11, God initiated a plan to cover people's sin of failing to obey the law (which kept them separated from Him). He said, "The life of the flesh is in the blood, and I have given it to you upon the altar to make atonement for your souls; for it is the blood that makes atonement for the soul" (NKJV).

The word atonement can be defined as a covering of sin. Since God knew it was impossible for the Israelites to obey all of His commands, He required a blood sacrifice. This practice promised to remove the stain of sin from God's sight. Without it, sin would continue to separate people from God, because "according to the law almost all things are purified with blood, and without shedding of blood there is no remission" (Hebrews 9:22 NKJV). So because nobody can fully obey all of the law all of the time, the blood covenant was established to remove sin from God's sight.

And I know I keep stressing "all of the law all of the time," but this is exactly the pressure the people were under if they wanted God's approval.

But that's not all. The law and the blood only temporarily made people right with God because "it's not possible that the blood of bulls and goats could take away sins" (Hebrews 10:4, NKJV). So the process of being made right with God became a continual cycle: obey the law, make atonement on the altar for the sin of not obeying, obey the law, make atonement on the altar for the sin of not obeying—repeat often.

Are you getting the picture? God had a plan with all of this, but if we were the ones under the old covenant, we too might be exhausted from all that work. (Or we might become perfectionists and a little proud of the part we could accomplish.)

Interestingly, synonyms for *work* are effort, exertion, labor, toil, and drudgery. Sounds like fun, huh?

But nevertheless, the Israelites were cursed if they didn't obey the instructions to "faithfully obey all these laws" (Deuteronomy 6:25, GW). They wanted to have the Lord's approval, but it was a lot of work. "For as many as are of the works of the law are under the curse; for it is written, 'Cursed is everyone who does *not continue* in all things which are written in the book of the law, to do them'" (Galatians 3:10 emphasis added, NKJV). So with good intentions, the people made every effort, exerting all their energy toward this one goal of being made righteous, all while suspecting that "no one can ever be made right in God's sight by doing what His law commands" (Romans 3:20, NKJV). Even now, the more we know God's law, the clearer it becomes that we aren't obeying it.

So the unmerited favor of God that we now know as grace was hoped for then, but it was not a surety. As a result, the people slowly began to change the rules and look to themselves for righteousness. It's human nature.

Good Job — Well Done

In 2 Samuel 22:21, King David said, "The LORD rewarded me according to my righteousness; according to the cleanness of my hands He has recompensed me" (NKJV). We know King David was found to be a man after God's own heart, so his statement was probably sincere. But David said God rewarded him according to "his" righteousness. This was true to the extent that God was pleased and did reward him for the right things he did. But any time we begin calling righteousness "ours," we're teetering on the edge of a dangerous cliff. Depending on our own ability to achieve righteousness is a close cousin to pride.

God has had to correct more than one person who "thought" they were righteous. For example, in Deuteronomy 9:6, Moses told all the people, "You must recognize that the LORD your God is not giving you this good land because you are good, for you are not—you are a stubborn people." In other words, the people became weary of obeying the law, and so when they did something good, they were naturally tempted to become haughty and a little resistant to God. They lived in a strict environment, so the more they followed the commandments, the more tempting it was to pat themselves on the back occasionally and say, "Good job! Well done." However, the problem with self-righteousness, or works-based faith, is that God receives less and less glory whenever man claims more.

And it's easy to become sympathetic to their situation because we all know it's natural for people to take credit for their work. "When people work, their wages are not a gift, but something they have earned" (Romans 4:4). But true righteousness (His favor and approval) is a gift from God, not payment for doing good. He desires to establish people in right-standing with Himself so He can have a relationship with them. He longs to have the same intimacy with us now that He had with Adam and Eve when He walked in close fellowship with them in the garden. And although man fell and the intimacy ended, God's desire never changed. In fact, in Leviticus 26:12, God said, "I will walk among you; and be your God, and you will be my people."

This has always been God's heart.

Because remember the law, the blood, and God's gift of righteousness were for one purpose: to re-establish that which had been broken. Yet, people "being ignorant of God's righteousness, and seeking to establish their own righteousness, have not submitted to the righteousness of God" (Romans 10:3, NKJV). This simply means, as the New Living Translation puts this same verse, "they don't understand God's way of making people right with himself. Refusing to accept God's way, they cling to their own way of getting right with God by trying to keep the law."

And this line of thinking perfectly sets the stage to answer the age-old question: What about Job?

The Can of Worms

Mentioning the book of Job is like opening a can of worms. Ask 12 people about the sufferings of Job, and you will easily find twelve opinions, all headed in different directions. However, when a can of worms is opened, something must be done with it. Therefore, before we look into the curious story of the man who challenged God, it's important to deal with a few of the issues and questions that tend to arise when Job's name is mentioned.

For starters, people have a hard time understanding a good God in the midst of a world full of suffering, afflictions, and pain. But all of this misery is the result of many things. For one, we have an enemy named Satan who has twisted and perverted our world with the intent of keeping people from ever knowing or hearing of Jesus Christ, their Redeemer. And although we might think that his destructive ways would push people toward a loving God, the devil has actually deceived many of us into believing that the world's pain and tragedies are part of God's doing. Yet God promises to be "a shelter for the oppressed, a refuge in times of trouble" (Psalm 9:9). But there's a hitch... this promise is to "those who know [His] name," to those who "put their trust in [Him]"; "For You, LORD, have not forsaken those who seek You" (Psalm 9:10, NKJV).

The point here is that God will never force any person to come to Him; it must be of their own doing. The psalmist said, "I will say of the LORD, 'He is my refuge and my fortress; My God, in Him I will trust'" (Psalm 91:2, NKJV). Notice that he said "I" will say of the Lord. It is the individual, free will of every person to find refuge in God. Their choice to seek Him cannot be made for them or forced upon them, not even by God Himself.

So another question arises: What about believers who have placed their trust in God? Many of them also suffer with pain, disease, and loss. Why is that? Shouldn't they be protected? The answer is both Yes and No. Jesus said, "These things I have spoken to you, that in Me you may have peace. In the world you will have tribulation; but be of good cheer, I have overcome the world" (John 16:33 NKJV). He never promised that we would not have adversity. In fact, the Scriptures teach just the opposite. But the adversity of believers comes with a promise. "Many are the afflictions of the righteous, but the LORD delivers him out of them all" (Psalm 34:19, NKJV).

The promise is not that we will never face affliction. The promise is that God will deliver us. But just as we have a part to play in coming to Him for salvation, we also have a responsibility to stay continually mindful of Him. "Those who live in the shelter of the Most High will find rest in the shadow of the Almighty," the psalmist assures us. Such a person can "declare about the LORD, 'He alone is my refuge, my place of safety; he is my God, and I trust him'" (Psalm 91:1–2). Those who make

God their dwelling place, by confessing Jesus as their Lord and then by continuing to walk in paths of righteousness, will find refuge, safety, and help.

But remember, God has given us the ability to choose where we walk. Therefore, it will always be the sole responsibility of every believer to stay unspotted from the world. If our choices move us outside of God's protection, then we may find ourselves open to attack and correction.

Attack or Correction?

When the Bible says, "Many are the afflictions of the righteous" (Psalm 34:19, NKJV), another question that arises is. Are the afflictions of the righteous an attack from our enemy, Satan, or are they simply correction from God?

Well, it depends. Many believe that the afflictions of the righteous are God's way of teaching us holiness. They point to passages like Hebrews 12:5–7:

> You have forgotten the exhortation which speaks to you as to sons: "My son, do not despise the chastening of the LORD, nor be discouraged when you are rebuked by Him; For whom the LORD loves He chastens, and scourges every son whom He receives." If you endure chastening, God deals with you as with sons; for what son is there whom a father does not chasten? (NKJV)

The <u>New Living Translation</u> tells us in verse 7: "As you endure this divine discipline, remember that God is treating you as His own children. Who ever heard of a child who never needed discipline?" But we need to be careful not to confuse discipline with abuse. If an earthly father breaks his child's leg to teach him a lesson, we don't call that discipline. Such a father would be punished severely for abusing his child. So the question remains: When bad things happen to Christians, is God just disciplining His children, or is He the one causing painful things to happen in order to teach them holiness or some other lesson?

Let me answer first by saying that because God loves us, He will correct us when we err. But Jesus said in John 10:10 that it is the thief who comes to "kill, steal, and destroy." He went on to say that He came to give us "life," and that "more abundantly." So God may be the one doing the disciplining, but He's never the one doing the killing, stealing, or destroying.

I recently looked up synonyms for the word destroy (words that mean the same thing), and I was surprised when I saw the list of antonyms (words that mean the complete opposite). The antonyms for destroy are author, creator, and restorer. All three of these are characteristics and names for God. This clearly points to the fact that God is *never* the destroyer.

In fact, when God corrects, it always come in the form of love, and we can thank Jesus for that. "For God presented Jesus as the sacrifice for sin. People are made right with God when they believe that Jesus sacrificed his life, shedding his blood.

This sacrifice shows that God was being fair when he held back and did not punish those who sinned in times past" (Romans 3:25). This passage stresses the fact that for centuries God "held back" and did not punish many of the sins of His people. He waited for the time when the blood of Jesus would make atonement for sin. Yes, He disciplines us, but everything He does is first motivated by His love to save us and help us—not hurt us.

The Sovereignty of God

To say God is the one causing believers to suffer, and then to declare, in the same breath, He is also the one who sets them free is nonsense. In fact, this kind of backwards thinking was addressed by Jesus when He was accused of doing the same. The Pharisees said of Him, "No wonder he can cast out demons. He gets his power from Satan, the prince of demons." But Jesus, knowing their thoughts, replied, "Any kingdom divided by civil war is doomed. A town or family splintered by feuding will fall apart. And if Satan is casting out Satan, he is divided and fighting against himself. His own kingdom will not survive" (Matthew 12:24–26).

The same would be true for God.

God's kingdom would never survive if He were doing both the afflicting and the delivering, yet He has been blamed for human suffering over and over. For example, when a young person dies, loved ones will say God needed them in heaven, and that is why God "took" him or her. Insurance companies have even labeled tornadoes, hurricanes, and other destructive forces as "acts of God," as if God Himself is the instigator of such destruction.

No, God's unquestioned sovereignty doesn't mean that everything that happens in our world is the will of God. For example, did God pick out the color of your shirt today or the breakfast you chose to eat (or not eat) this morning? Of course not. The Lord has given you and me free will to make decisions. All kinds of decisions. And these decisions, when multiplied by millions of people, set the course for our world. It's incredible, isn't it, that the Creator of this earth would let us run it so much of the time?

Not only do we get a large say about things, but when man fell in the Garden of Eden, much of the authority now governing our world was given to Satan. When the devil tempted Jesus to bow down and worship him, the tempter flaunted this dominion, saying, "All this authority I will give You . . . ; for this has been delivered to me, and I give it to whomever I wish" (Luke 4:6, NKJV). Of course, Jesus didn't give in to this ridiculous temptation, but the fact remains the devil paraded his influence over the kingdoms of the world in front of Jesus simply because he could.

So if God's sovereignty means He is in control of everything that happens, Jesus would have responded quite differently. Instead, He acknowledged the truth of what Satan said and answered, "Get behind Me, Satan! For it is written, 'You shall worship the LORD your God, and Him only you shall serve'"

(Luke 4:8, NKJV). Satan was given control of the earth, and Jesus referred to him as "the ruler of this world" in at least three different places: John 12:31; 14:30; and 16:11.

The bottom line is that it's the devil who is a liar and a thief, and the bad guy on this stage doing the killing, stealing, and destroying—not God. But we know God's sovereignty is not limited by the temporary power of Satan. The power of God is absolute. His sovereignty is to His Word. God is "not a man that He should lie" (Numbers 23:19, NKJV), therefore His word is utmost, supreme, and greatest in degree—all of which are definitions of sovereignty. Therefore, because God is all-powerful (sovereign), His Word always accomplishes His purpose.

As the rain comes down, and the snow from heaven, And do not return there, But water the earth, And make it bring forth and bud, That it may give seed to the sower And bread to the eater, So shall My word be that goes forth from My mouth; It shall not return to Me void, But it shall accomplish what I please, And it shall prosper in the thing for which I sent it.

(Isaiah 55:10–11 NKJV)

Found in God's word is both His promise and His ability to move on behalf of His children—including delivering them from evil when they call upon Him.

Persecution and Sin

Whatever we formulate as an explanation of sovereignty, the inescapable truth remains that believers will continue to endure suffering and affliction for two main reasons: (1) persecution for righteousness and (2) consequence for sin. But in neither case is God the source of the affliction. In fact, concerning persecution, the apostle Paul said:

> We proudly tell God's other churches about your endurance and faithfulness in all the persecutions and hardships you are suffering. But God will use this persecution to show his justice and to make you worthy of his Kingdom, for which you are suffering. In his justice he will pay back those who persecute you.
>
> (2 Thessalonians 1:4–6)

Living a righteous life is no easy task because it invites persecution from all who do not believe. But Paul said God would use this to show His justice. In other words, in this life, believers may face harassing and oppressive treatment, and, at times, it will involve suffering and affliction. But remember, we do not wrestle against flesh and blood, but against principalities and powers of darkness (Ephesians 6:12). God is not our enemy. The kingdom of light is at war with the kingdom of darkness. And the Bible says the devil roams about like a roaring lion, seeking whom he may devour (1 Peter 5:8).

The flip side of affliction from persecution is the inevitable consequences of sin. The Scriptures tell us, "There will be trouble and calamity for everyone who keeps on doing what is evil—for the Jew first and also for the Gentile" (Romans 2:9). Christians who open the back door in their lives for Satan through sin will face some tribulation—either in the form of discipline, which is never fun, or through an outright attack by Satan.

It isn't something we easily acknowledge, but much of our pain in this life is the result of our own transgressions, whether individually or worldwide. When we step away from the refuge and safety of our God and set foot in the devil's playground, we are exposed to Satan's booby-traps and irregular rounds of ammunition, both of which he loves to use in his arena.

Satan doesn't know the intents of people's hearts. He is not omniscient like God. He is pure darkness, and his only goal is to snuff out the light carried about in the hearts of men and women who belong to God. In other words, Satan doesn't have to know you personally—he recognizes you because of your light. Therefore, Christians who decide to live outside the protection of the Almighty are prey to Satan's attacks and fair game for destruction.

So regardless of whether affliction for believers is the result of persecution or because of sin, the bottom line is that we can find refuge when we turn to God. And Job is the perfect example of this.

Through adversity, we learn to overcome. Jesus said, "To him who overcomes I will grant to sit with Me on My throne, as I also overcame and sat down with My Father on His throne" (Revelation 3:21, NKJV). The repeated experiences of overcoming trains us to put our trust in God instead of ourselves and ensures that all the glory remains with Him. So, although we could discuss at some length the topics of God's sovereignty and the sufferings and affliction of believers, that is not the purpose of this book. But in preparing the foundation for the thoughts that will follow, these ideas needed to be examined.

Christians have always faced suffering and affliction. They always will. But none of us more so than Job. However, before we come to any conclusions, let us look together into this tale of the man who challenged God to find some answers.

CHAPTER TWO
Read Job, Chapters 1-3

In the Life of Job

A certain gentleman went to a barbershop to get a haircut. While he was there, he and the barber made small talk about everything from politics to religion. The barber commented that he didn't believe there was a God. "How can there be?" he asked. "If there is a God, then why is there so much pain and suffering in our world? What kind of God would allow His people to hurt?"

The fellow in the chair didn't know how to answer the barber. In his own heart, he believed God was real, but he too had wondered about the pain and suffering in the world and what purpose it served.

Observing the barber's demeanor, he decided it would be fruitless to argue, so he said nothing. After paying for his haircut, he stepped outside to go to his car. As he began to cross the street, he noticed a homeless man, unshaven with wild hair, pushing a shopping cart filled with what seemed to be his life's belongings. The gentleman quickly turned around and went back into the barbershop. Looking the barber squarely in the eyes, he said, "You know, maybe there's no such thing as barbers."

The barber was quite puzzled by the man's comment. "That's silly," he retorted. "I'm one."

The gentleman then pointed out the window at the homeless man and said, "Oh really? Just look at that man."

The barber laughed sarcastically and replied, "Well, that doesn't mean barbers don't exist—that man just doesn't come to me for help." To which, the gentleman responded, "I believe that's God's problem too."

I Know Your Works

Self-righteousness is an attempt to meet God's standard based upon one's own merit. In the story of the barber, the gentleman realizes God is available to all who call upon Him. Therefore, is it fair to blame God if people trust in themselves instead of taking advantage of His help? When we begin to look to ourselves for help (instead of God), we inadvertently move away from Him and His provision. And moving away from God moves us closer to His enemy, Satan.

In the book of Revelation, Jesus told John to write down messages to the angels of seven churches. It's interesting to study what was written to the church of the Laodiceans. He said, "I know your works that you are neither cold nor hot. I could wish you were cold or hot. So then, because you are lukewarm, and neither cold nor hot, I will vomit you out of My mouth. Because you say, 'I am rich, have become wealthy, and have need of nothing'—and do not know that you are wretched, miserable, poor, blind, and naked . . ." (Revelations 3:15–17 NKJV).

Looking back on my own life, it wasn't until I walked through some hard times that I discovered how much I naturally depended on myself—and how little I trusted and depended on God. But He knew. And although I thought I had it all together, the truth was that I was "wretched, miserable, poor, blind, and naked."

For this reason, God often allows us to walk through adversities—not so He can see what we are made of, He already knows—He allows it so that we can see what we are made of.

My Servant Job

This is where we enter the story of Job. According to Scripture:

Job was a man who lived in Uz. He was honest inside and out, a man of his word, who was totally devoted to God and hated evil with a passion. He had seven sons and three daughters. He was also very wealthy—seven thousand head of sheep, three thousand camels, five hundred teams of oxen, five hundred donkeys, and a huge staff of servants—the most influential man in all the East!

His sons used to take turns hosting parties in their homes, always inviting their three sisters to join them in their merrymaking. When the parties were over, Job would get up early in the morning and sacrifice a burnt offering for each of his children, thinking, "Maybe one of them sinned by defying God inwardly." Job made a habit of this sacrificial atonement, just in case they'd sinned.

(Job 1:1–5, MSG)

To say Job was the most influential man "in all the East" might be an understatement. The description of his wealth in the form of sheep, camels, donkeys, and oxen alone would describe something like an *Ameer*, or *Arabian prince*, someone with notable power and persuasion, to say the least. We're not told how he obtained this great wealth, whether by inheritance or hard labor, but it is clear that Job was a blessed man by any standard.

It's almost funny to read about the parties his children would throw with Dad's money. In fact, one translation says, "His sons would go and feast in their houses, each on his appointed day" (Job 1:4, NKJV). In other words, they celebrated their birthdays with big bashes! So big, in fact, that the celebration apparently wasn't just one day but "days of feasting." Now multiply that times seven sons and three daughters. We get the picture of a lengthy party almost every month of the year—or at least enough that Job felt it necessary to pray and offer sacrifices for his kids' craziness.

In the past, we have taken our family and a few of my son's teenaged friends out to eat and to the movies for his birthday. Just for one night of celebration, we've spent several hundred dollars, so it's not hard to imagine spending thousands upon thousands of dollars for a week or more of feasting with family and friends. Now multiply that by at least ten times every year (one for each child)—and that's if the kids only celebrated their birthdays—and we've got a pretty good glimpse of the lavish living Job's children were accustomed to.

Yes, Job was well taken care of. We haven't even looked at what it might have cost to provide for his large staff. But just imagining fields full of thousands of sheep, and thousands of camels, and thousands of oxen and donkeys is enough data for us to realize that Job had a hefty payroll. He was a man of means—a princely shepherd—and one who followed God's law faithfully.

Yet, one day when the angels went to present themselves to the Lord, Satan went with them. God inquired as to where he had come from, and Satan replied he had been on the earth. "Have you considered My servant Job, that there is none like him on the earth, a blameless and upright man, one who fears God and shuns evil?" God asked (1:8, NKJV). We've often read God's question, "Have you considered My servant Job?" as if God was bragging on Job. But the primary meaning of word *considered* in the original language is to put, to set, or to place.[2] Therefore, since God is omniscient, He is really saying, "You've been considering my servant Job, haven't you?" In other words, God knew Satan had set his heart on him.

Unimpressed (and most likely guilty), Satan responded that any person God protected and blessed so lavishly would serve Him and stay away from evil. "But reach out and take away everything he has, and he will surely curse you to your face" (1:11)! Satan was pretty confident that the heart of man would always be more loyal to his possessions and family than to God. Proverbs 21:2 tells us that "every way of a man is right in his own eyes, but the LORD weighs the hearts" (NKJV). And knowing the hidden things of Job's heart, God allowed Satan to attack his property and family. "All right, you may test him," the Lord said to Satan. "Do whatever you want with everything he possesses, but don't harm him physically" (1:12). That's all the permission Satan needed—or was it? The New King James Version says, "Behold, all that he has is in your power." (We'll soon find out why this statement is so important.)

Seemingly without notice, as the servants and animals are in the field and the children are hosting yet another party with Dad's money, one messenger after another comes running up to Job with awful news of destruction and calamity striking his servants, his property, and eventually his children. "Your oxen were plowing, with the donkeys feeding beside them, when the Sabeans raided us. They stole all the animals and killed all the farmhands. I am the only one who escaped to tell you," one servant reported. Then the door of the tent burst open with another frantic message: "The fire of God has fallen from heaven and burned up your sheep and all the shepherds. I am the only one who escaped to tell you." And then, to Job's utter disbelief, a third messenger came running up. "Three bands of Chaldean raiders have stolen your camels and killed your servants," he announced. "I am the only one who escaped to tell you" (1:14–17).

Imagine the shock Job must have been feeling. He'd just been told all his wealth vanished. Probably half in shock and half in skepticism, Job ran outside to see for himself the horrors reported to him. But running up the path comes yet another messenger, out of breath and with tears streaming down his face. "Your sons and daughters were feasting in their oldest brother's home," he cried to Job. "Suddenly, a powerful wind swept in from the wilderness and hit the house on all sides. The house collapsed, and all your children are dead. I am the only one who escaped to tell you" (1:18).

We can only guess the thoughts that must have run through Job's head. Crushed and overcome with grief, his whole psyche must have been screaming, *How? Why? What?* Then, doing what he knew to do—what he trained himself to do—Job stood and tore his robe in grief. Then he shaved his head and fell to the ground to worship. He prayed, "I came naked from my mother's womb, and I will be naked when I leave. The Lord gave me what I had, and the Lord has taken it away. Praise the name of the Lord" (1:21)! And the first chapter of Job's story ends with the Bible telling us, "In all of this, Job did not sin by blaming God" (1:22).

Skin for Skin

Soon afterward, we find Satan returning to God after roaming the earth. Again the Lord questioned him, asking him if he'd been considering his servant Job. The obvious answer was Yes, but Satan still was not impressed with Job's endurance or integrity. "Skin for skin! A man will give up everything to save his life" (2:4)! Satan had been wrong about Job's loyalty to his possessions and family, but he was convinced that if a man's health was on the line, he would surely curse God. This time, however, the Lord put limits on Satan, "Behold, he is in your hand; only spare his life" (2:6, AMP). So Satan struck Job with painful boils from head to toe; so painful that Job's only relief was to sit and lance the boils with broken pieces of pottery.

He must have been a pitiful sight, for his wife said to him, "Are you still trying to maintain your integrity? Curse God and die." But Job replied, "You talk like a foolish woman. Should we accept only good things from the hand of God and never anything bad?" What an interesting reply...

Many people have commended Job for correcting his wife. But is this really the point Scripture is trying to make? Christians go through the motions every day, saying and doing the right thing because that is what they've been trained to do. God said Job was blameless. But it's important to note there are many Bible scholars who claim the book of Job was written before the flood, and therefore before the Mosaic law was handed out, so it's assumed the law doesn't affect the context here. However, Romans 2:14–15 says, "Whenever non-Jews who don't have the laws in Moses' Teachings do by nature the things that those laws contain, they are a law to themselves even though they don't have any of those laws. They show that some requirements found in Moses' Teachings are written in their hearts. Their consciences speak to them. Their thoughts accuse them on one occasion and defend them on another." (GW).

Somehow Job has learned to follow a set of prescribed laws that honor God—which seems to include something resembling the third commandment, which says you are not to take the name of the Lord your God in vain. So to curse God, as Job's wife suggested, would have been against what Job knew to be right. But let's not forget, God can see what we can't. His Word says, "As in water face reflects face, so a man's heart reveals the man" (Proverbs 27:19, NKJV).

"So in all this, Job said nothing wrong" (2:9–10). Another translation says Job "did not sin with his lips" (NKJV).

Letting Our Guard Down

Now Job's story takes an interesting twist. Three of Job's friends were Eliphaz, Bildad, and Zophar. When they heard of the tragedy he had suffered, "they got together and traveled from their homes to comfort and console him. Then they sat on the ground with him for seven days and nights. No one said a word to Job, for they saw that his suffering was too great for words" (2:11, 13). Job's friends came to comfort him, but seeing the severity of his adversities, they didn't know what to say. It is likely that they, too, had been taught the essence of the law and were being careful. Remember the gentleman in the barbershop story didn't know how to respond either. The danger with silence, however, is that it can be interpreted as agreement.

Initially, Job didn't want to blame God, but sometimes when we are with those closest to us, we tend to let our guard down and speak more freely from our hearts.

At last Job spoke, and he cursed the day of his birth. He said: "Let the day of my birth be erased, and the night I was conceived. Curse that day for failing to shut my mother's womb, for letting me be born to see all this trouble. Why wasn't I buried like a stillborn child, like a baby who never lives to see the light? For in death the wicked cause no trouble, and the weary are at rest. Even captives are at ease in death, with no guards to curse them. Rich and poor are both there, and the slave is free from his master. Oh, why give light to those in misery, and life to those who are bitter? They long for death, and it won't come. They search for death more eagerly than for hidden treasure. They're filled with joy when they finally die, and rejoice when they find the grave."

(3:1–3, 10, 16–22)

Out of the abundance of the heart, Job's mouth finally spoke. What he'd been meditating on for seven days was exposed. Originally, he said, "Shall we accept only good from God and not bad?" But notice what happened when adversity came and stayed a little while—how quickly our hearts and our thoughts are revealed. Job said he wished for death, but in actuality, he wanted understanding. And considering his current state, maybe Job wanted both, but as we'll soon discover, he definitely wanted justification for what had happened to him.

As a side note, it's very important for us to realize that not every statement in the book of Job expresses God's heart and mind. We are reading the *conversations* of a confused and hurt man who was surrounded by men as wrong as he was. But sadly, because what we are studying is Bible text, some people take Job's statements and assume they are gospel truth. Many of the scriptures in this story are his emotions. And yes, they are recorded just as they were said—they are a true account of his statements—but this does not necessarily mean that they contain God's truth.

When people take scriptures such as the ones we will be looking at and, instead of reading them in context of the story, make them a doctrine, they can wind up teaching and believing some erroneous things. In this case, they may believe that because Job said it, it must be true that every bad thing that happens in a Christian's life is God doing it for some reason.

As we continue our study of the story of Job, please keep your heart and mind open regarding the thoughts and discussions presented here. When we reach the end of the story, we'll find out what God has to say.

The First Indicator

The truth is we all have flesh, and our flesh has a voice. Even Paul said in Romans 7:15–17, "I don't really understand myself, for I want to do what is right, but I don't do it. Instead, I do what I hate. But if I know that what I am doing is wrong, this shows that I agree that the law is good. So I am not the one doing wrong; it is sin living in me that does it." Paul said it well. It is the inherited sin nature in each of us that wants to have its way and its say.

Some would argue Job isn't sinning here, stating he's just angry over what's happened to him. It is true he is upset, but the Bible says in James 1:19-20, "So then, my beloved brethren, let every man be swift to hear, slow to speak, slow to wrath; for the wrath of man does not produce the righteousness of God" (NKJV). The truth is we all get angry, but there is a definite link between speaking angrily from the flesh and slipping into sin (that which doesn't produce the righteousness of God).

God wants us to speak honestly with Him (and some prayers are honest venting with God), but we mustn't forget there's a line between honesty and disrespect. Disrespect is a sin of the heart and is often the result of anger on the part of the one hurting. And at this point in our story, Job has not recognized that it is his sin nature talking. He is angry and simply saying what he feels. And often, this is the first mistake we all make.

Faith and feelings are two different things. If our faith is tied to our feelings—which will constantly change based on our circumstances—then our faith will go up and down like a roller coaster. However, if our faith is in God, then regardless of what our *flesh* wants to say, *our faith* will override it, or at least be quick to repent. In an adverse way, however, trusting in our feelings opens us up to the enemy and his deception.

Obviously, our faith should always be based on God's word and God's true character. Emotions aren't all bad, but to live by our emotions is contrary to Scripture (not to mention dangerous). Romans 1:17 says that God's righteousness is revealed from *faith* to *faith* (not feeling to feeling). If only Job could have gotten this same revelation sooner.

Notice what he said next: "What I always feared has happened to me. What I dreaded has come true" (3:25). The New King James Version words it this way: "For the thing I greatly feared has come upon me, and what I dreaded has happened to me." This is a sad statement because this kind of fear is never from God; "For God has not given us a spirit of fear, but of power and of love and of a sound mind" (2 Timothy 1:7, NKJV). Fear (and it's author, Satan) is the number one tormenter of all humans.

Job wasn't saying he was *now* afraid. He said what he *always* feared (what had always been in the crevices of his heart) had come upon him. Job is being honest about his phobias. And it's good to be honest with God when we're worried or afraid, but the lesson here is the past tense of Job's statement: "What I always feared has happened to me." It's important to deal with our fears quickly, lest the fear itself opens the door for greater torment or attack at the hand of Satan.

As our story unfolds, we'll learn something else about fear: When we become dependent on our works (our best ability to accomplish something on our own), an element of fear will always be involved because of human error.

Job's statement of fear is actually our first indicator of some self-righteousness—his attempt to meet God's standards based upon his own merits. If righteousness is right-standing with God, then "self" righteousness is our attempt to do it ourselves. Many times, we see the word *self-righteousness* and think it must be evil, when in all actuality, it often stems from a heart that wants desperately to please God but doesn't know how to do so by faith.

Job was a man who loved God and wanted to please Him. Job 1:1 says he was "blameless and upright, and one who feared God and shunned evil" (NKJV). His prayers and sacrifices were proof of this. But Job was also human. Whether he ever admitted it or not, he knew there was always room for human error. And it invites fear when you are prone to doing things by the letter of the law.

The underlying message of this book is revealing self-righteousness and defending God's character. Jesus said the Holy Spirit (within us) would convict the world of sin, and of righteousness, and of judgment (John 16:8). When we ignore the Holy Spirit, His conviction can be misdiagnosed. This is often how self-righteousness shows up and why "fear" is real. It should always be a big indicator for us that something's wrong—because God is not the author of fear.

Our flesh is corrupt and full of flaws, and our spirit knows it. On the outside, we can act blameless and upright, but deep down inside, an inward voice can be trying to warn us. But if we have any self-righteous tendencies (even with good intent), we may not recognize the warning and instead, intuitively call it fear, which is exactly what Job did.

So reliance on our ability to be made right by our works breeds an internal apprehension in us, because we know that if we make a mistake, it's really our own fault for trusting in ourselves more than we should. Isaiah said, "The poor, deluded fool feeds on ashes. He trusts something that can't help him at all.

Yet he cannot bring himself to ask, 'Is this idol that I'm holding in my hand a lie'?" (44:20)

Idol worship is simply trusting in anything other than God. So trusting in our own ability to be made righteous is an empty act of wrong worship, and often unknowingly, it opens us up to anxieties and misgivings (and more opportunities for Satan), because trusting in ourselves amounts to trusting in something that can never help us.

CHAPTER THREE
Read Job, Chapters 4-7

The Deception

Self-righteousness is self-deception and deception is reality minus the truth.

None of us would believe an outright, obvious lie. But mix a little reality with the lie and we might fall for it. In Hosea 4:6, God said, "My people are destroyed for lack of knowledge" (NKJV). This lets Satan take advantage of us. He can deceive us by speaking reality minus the truth. And if we don't know the truth, we'll believe the lie based on the deception.

God Is Not the Culprit

When Job cursed the day of his birth, it revealed he didn't know the truth about why he was hurting so horribly. Earlier he had said, "Should we accept only good things from the hand of God and never anything bad?" This statement alone revealed deception. Job didn't understand the character of God.

Years ago, the Lord gave me a great example of this. When my oldest son was a preteen, he had a problem keeping his room clean (like most teenagers). However, it never crossed my mind to go into his room while he was at school and trash it just so I could teach him a lesson. But if he, on his own, allowed his room to get in a total mess, I had no problem letting him spend some time cleaning it up in hopes he would see the need to keep it in order.

In the same way, just like I would never purposely destroy my son's room, God doesn't need to cause bad things to happen to us just to teach us a lesson. Job said, "Should we accept only good things from the hand of God and never anything bad?" as if God is the one who causes bad things to happen to us. No, on the contrary, if we move away from God and open the door to the enemy, whose only desire is to destroy us, God may allow us to walk through that door (with Him) so we can gain knowledge and see the truth. And when we know the truth, Satan's ability to take advantage of us is reduced.

The reason so many people, like Job, have believed God goes against His proven nature of goodness to cause harm is deception. Nothing makes Satan happier than taking glory away from God. The *truth* is God doesn't need to trash our lives to teach us anything. He loves us, and wants to help us. Our God is not the author of chaos, confusion, disorder, pain, grief, or death. All of these are contrary to His nature.

"Let no one say when he is tempted, 'I am tempted by God'; for God cannot be tempted by evil, nor does He Himself tempt anyone [with evil]... Do not be deceived, my beloved brethren.

Every good gift and every perfect gift is from above, and comes down from the Father of lights, with whom there is no variation or shadow of turning" (James 1:13,16–17 NKJV, paraphrase added). The Message says it best: "There is nothing deceitful in God, nothing two-faced, nothing fickle."

The problem with thinking God is the perpetrator of harm is that it goes against God's true character, as the story of Job reveals.

During those seven days of silence, it is likely Satan sat and whispered accusations against God in Job's ear. Hasn't He done that to you—slinging thoughts of accusation against God onto the walls of your mind? Satan's goal is to get God's people to believe things about the Lord that are contrary to His true nature.

When Job broke the silence by cursing the day of his birth, his friends were a bit alarmed and had their own thoughts to share. Eliphaz was the first to speak up:

> In the past you have encouraged many people; you have strengthened those who were weak. Your words have supported those who were failing; you have encouraged those with shaky knees. But now when trouble strikes, you lose heart. You are terrified when it touches you.
>
> Doesn't your reverence for God give you confidence? Doesn't your life of integrity give you hope?
>
> (4:3–6)

Who Said That?

Eliphaz asks some sincere questions, but the Bible says Satan is the accuser of the brethren. So when we yield to him, he can use us to accuse one another. His goal is to multiply the deception and cast doubt on God.

As Eliphaz continued, his questions actually begin to question: If Job were right with God, would all of these things have happened? He continues his probing by saying,

> This truth was given to me in secret, as though whispered in my ear. . . . In the silence I heard a voice say, 'Can a mortal be innocent before God? Can a person be pure before the Creator?" If God does not trust his own angels and has charged his messengers with foolishness, how much less will he trust people made of clay! They are made of dust, crushed as easily as a moth.
>
> (4:12, 16–19)

Someone whispered in his ear alright, but it wasn't the voice of truth. Satan is the one having a heyday whispering evil against God in Eliphaz's ear, for he himself was one of the angels God could not trust and charged with error.

Eliphaz clearly doesn't have good discernment regarding God's character, any more than Job does, or he would have recognized the lies of Satan and resisted those thoughts. Instead, he erroneously implies that God doesn't care about His children and will crush them if they make a mistake. Yet Psalm 33:15 says, "[God] made their hearts, so he understands everything they do." In other words, nothing is a surprise to God. He knows we have a sinful nature prone to error.

Let's be clear: God doesn't make excuses for our sins, but He doesn't crush us because of them either.

A Tainted View

Eliphaz thinks he knows why all these calamities have fallen on Job.

Surely resentment destroys the fool, and jealousy kills the simple. I have seen that fools may be successful for the moment, but then comes sudden disaster. But evil does not spring from the soil, and trouble does not sprout from the earth. People are born for trouble as readily as sparks fly up from a fire. If I were you, I would go to God and present my case to him. He does great things too marvelous to understand. He performs countless miracles. But consider the joy of those corrected by God! Do not despise the discipline of the Almighty when you sin. For though he wounds, he also bandages. He strikes, but his hands also heal.

(5:2–3, 6–9, 17–18)

Elements of truth are intermingled in Eliphaz's words. Resentment does destroy a fool, and jealousy can kill the simple. And God does do amazing works too marvelous to understand—yes, He even performs miracles without number. God is pleased when we know His character and walk in truth (3 John 4 NKJV). But the problem with deception is that we often don't know *enough* truth to keep us from being deceived.

Mixed with Eliphaz's truths about God are also his misunderstandings. "People are born for trouble as predictably as sparks fly upward from a fire." "For though he wounds, he also bandages. He strikes, but his hands also heal." It is sad that some people view God in this light. My question is: Did God create us to destroy us?

Belief System Challenged

And how will Job respond? He replied to Eliphaz:

If my misery could be weighed and my troubles be put on the scales, they would outweigh all the sands of the sea. That is why I spoke impulsively. For the Almighty has struck me down with his arrows. Their poison infects my spirit. God's terrors are lined against me.

(6:1–4)

Job is in a bad state. Satan has attacked him, and now everything he ever secretly feared about God has been exposed. Is this why he followed God's law so carefully? Was he afraid of God's wrath? Oh that God's people would worship and obey him in spirit and truth and not out of fear!

Job's next comment was a little humorous, but it sounded like most of us. "Don't I have a right to complain? Don't wild donkeys bray when they find no grass, and oxen bellow when they have no food?" (6:5). At first he said he wouldn't curse God. Then he said he'd accept the good and the bad from God. Now after thinking about it, Job decides he at least has a right to complain. But do any of us ever have a "right" to complain? I know bad things happen, but we have to be careful. Complaining kept the children of Israel in the wilderness for 40 years versus the estimated trip of only 11 days (according to Deuteronomy 1:2). Complaining is also related to self-justification, which is an important point to note. For example, King Saul was removed as king because he justified his actions by blaming others (1 Samuel 15). Job's life had been turned upside-down but there's a reason—and it's not because God was bored and decided to have target practice on Job—which is exactly why Job (or any of us) need to be careful when we feel we have a "right" to complain.

Another lesson here is that any time we change our mind regarding our theology (without it being based on revelation from God's word), we should stop and consider why. Flip-flopping so easily in our thoughts and beliefs may be a sign that we are not walking in the fullness of truth. And this is why adversities can be good for us. They reveal what we really believe.

If our belief system is never challenged, we might be walking in deception but never know it. This might be another reason why God allows us to walk through hard times, again not so He can see what we are made of but so that we can learn from our mistakes and avoid future pitfalls.

No Excuses

As Job continued his defense, more of his belief system was revealed.

I wish he would crush me. I wish he would reach out his hand and kill me. At least I can take comfort in this: Despite the pain, I have not denied the words of the Holy One.

(6:9–10)

More warning signs: self-righteousness is self-deception—and self-deception is self-justification.

The Message Translation states: "Let God step on me—squash me like a bug, and be done with me for good. I'd at least have the satisfaction of not having blasphemed the Holy God..." Job wished God would go ahead and kill him, but then he asserted some defense wanting everyone to know that *if* God killed him, He would do it unjustly.

Job's self-righteous words here don't make him a bad person; they make him human. We've all done the same thing at some point, but that doesn't mean it's okay (or approved) by

God. Job has a wrong view of God's character but thinks because he's never denied God's Word it means he's not wrong. The reason all of us have to mature in Christ is because we have wrong mindsets. And as we grow in revelation of what God calls right and wrong (including issues of the heart), we make the necessary adjustments growing from faith to faith. But at this point in our story, Job isn't aware he needs to make any adjustments—he just wants to be justified.

So Job continues to defend himself and challenge his friends:

One should be kind to a fainting friend, but you accuse me without any fear of the Almighty. You, too, have given no help. You have seen my calamity, and you are afraid.

Teach me, and I will keep quiet. Show me what I have done wrong. Honest words can be painful, but what do your criticisms amount to? Do you think your words are convincing when you disregard my cry of desperation? Stop assuming my guilt, for I have done no wrong.

(6:14, 21, 24–26, 29)

A common defense mechanism all of us have is the desire to vindicate and excuse ourselves. The number one way we tend to do this is by turning the tables on our accuser. Job doesn't recognize his own fears, but he clearly sees them in Eliphaz. Yet his argument for justice only revealed his own belief that he had done nothing wrong. "Stop assuming my guilt, for I have done no wrong."

As we follow the conversations of Job, it's important to note the timeline of revelation by Job himself. Here it would seem Job is speaking the truth about being righteous (being right versus being wrong). However, as later chapters discuss, there's a difference between the law of righteousness (works, pride, etc.) and the righteousness of faith (the gift of Christ which is not based on any of our own doing). And this is the case for self-righteousness: when people believe they can't possibly be guilty of anything.

God said Job was blameless. But blameless is not the same as being perfect (without sin)—yet the repeated defense by many people regarding Job is that he couldn't have had sin because God said he was blameless (or righteous). Can you see the flaw in this line of thinking? The original Hebrew word used to describe Job in chapter 1 is the word tām, meaning integrity and completeness. The *Complete Word Study Bible* says, "This is a rare, almost exclusively poetic term often translated perfect but not carrying the sense of totally free from fault, for it was used of quite flawed people. It describes the mild manner of Jacob in contrast to his brother Esau, who was characterized by shedding blood. The term often carries a rather strong moral component in certain contexts and appears among a list of glowing terms describing the admirable qualities of the

Shulamite lover."[3] In other words, Job was a man just like you and me. He was loved by God and had great qualities, but he was also a flawed human and therefore susceptible to the same traps and pitfalls of the flesh we all face.

And in his flawed condition, Job turned his accusations toward God:

> I cannot keep from speaking. I must express my anguish. My bitter soul must complain. I hate my life and I don't want to go on living. Oh, leave me alone for my few remaining days. What are people, that you should make so much of us, that you should think of us so often? For you examine us every morning and test us every moment. Why won't you leave me alone at least long enough for me to swallow! If I have sinned, what have I done to you, O watcher of all humanity? Why make me your target? Am I a burden to you?
>
> (7:11, 16–20)

I often tell my children that a bad attitude will get them in trouble quicker than their actual words. Sometimes it is not so much *what* we say, but *how* we say it.

If Job thought it possible to be in the wrong (even if he didn't know what he had done), then a heart of remorse would have been exposed. But to the contrary, Job's attitude was proud, arrogant, and over-confident. It's actually scary how sarcastic his words were: "What have I done to you, O watcher of all humanity?" Another translation says, "Therefore I will not restrain my mouth; I will speak in the anguish of my spirit, I will complain in the bitterness of my soul" (NKJV). In Job's own confession we find more proof that not everything he is said was the truth about God. Job said he was speaking from anguish, not truth.

We can't blame Job for being angry, but it's important to point out that in his current belief system, he was perfect and God was wrong. Job just stated he had a right to complain in the bitterness of his soul. This phrase, "O watcher of all humanity" is as bitter as they come… and bitterness is sin.

What's scariest, however, is Job's lack of excuses for his attitude. He knew what he was doing and he didn't care. Oh, how often have we done the same thing? It is the way of all flesh.

CHAPTER FOUR

Read Job, Chapters 8-13

Ugly Emotions

There's a lot of truth in this proverb: "Before destruction the heart of a man is haughty, and before honor is humility" (Proverbs 18:12, NKJV). Haughtiness is a word used to describe great pride in oneself, and disdain, contempt, or scorn for others. On the other hand, humility is lowliness of mind, meaning the humble do not think more highly of themselves than they should. Humility is an attitude that places glory in its proper place. For example, Isaiah 2:11 says, "The day is coming when your proud looks will be brought low; the LORD alone will be exalted" (TLB).

At a moment, Job's attitude was not that of a humble man. He had taken great pride in his ability to follow a prescribed set of godly laws, which was why Eliphaz was unable to reason with Him in his first attempt. But it didn't help that Eliphaz's own understanding of God's character was just as flawed.

But maybe one of Job's other friends could help.

The Boomerang

Then Bildad . . . replied to Job: How long will you go on like this? Your sound like a blustering wind. Does God twist justice? Does the Almighty twist what is right? Your children must have sinned against him, so their punishment was well deserved. But if you pray to God and seek the favor of the Almighty, and if you are pure and live with integrity, he will surely rise up and restore your happy home. But look! God will not reject a person of integrity, nor will he lend a hand to the wicked.

(8:1–6, 20)

Sadly, we see flaws in Bildad's perception of God as well. He too seemed to think God was a lightning bolt in heaven waiting to strike. He was right to say God lifts up those of integrity and that ultimately evildoers will find no prosperity, but Bildad was also implying that Job must be an evildoer and that God is going to get him! This is the kind of warped thinking the devil wants us to believe about God.

But one thing Bildad said triggers a different kind of response from Job. For a moment, he remembered that God alone is just.

Then Job spoke again: "Yes, I know all this is true in principle. But how can a person be declared innocent in God's sight? If someone wanted to take God to court, would it be possible to answer him even once in a thousand times? So who am I, that I should try to answer God or even reason with him? Even if I were right, I would have no defense. I could only plead for mercy."

(9:1–3, 14–15)

For a moment, it appeared that Job was letting go of his pride. But pride can be an ugly boomerang; when released, it just comes back around and hits us square in the face.

Impurities Rise First

Job acknowledged that God was judge and jury, and therefore just. But his defense wasn't ready to soften.

Though I am innocent, my own mouth would pronounce me guilty. Though I am blameless, it would prove me wicked. Innocent or wicked, it is all the same to God. That's why I say, "He destroys both the blameless and the wicked." When a plague sweeps through, he laughs at the death of the innocent. If I decided to forget my complaints, to put away my sad face and be cheerful, I would still dread all the pain, for I know you will not find me innocent, O God. Whatever happens, I will be found guilty. So what's the use of trying?

(9:20, 22–23, 27–29)

Oh, how "the lips of the wise disperse knowledge, but the heart of the fool does not do so!" (Proverbs 15:7 NKJV). It is regrettable that Job views God in such a dark light. But as with anything being purified, the impurities always rise to the surface first. Every misconception Job has ever held in his heart now rises up out of his mouth. This is another good example of something we can learn from Job's story. Again, Job's honesty doesn't make him (or anyone else) a bad person. But the things that come out of our mouths are always an indicator of what's been hiding in our heart—right or wrong.

And then from Job's own mouth, in the midst of his rambling emotions, comes what sounds almost like a prophecy of our Redeemer, "If only there were a mediator between us, someone who could bring us together. The mediator could make God stop beating me, and I would no longer live in terror of his punishment" (9:33–34).

Job is still wrong in his perception of God. He should never feel like he has to live in terror of God. But God isn't oblivious to Satan's goal to pervert man's heart into believing He's merciless. This is one reason God knew in advance we would need a mediator; "For there is one God and one Mediator between God and men, the Man Christ Jesus" (1 Timothy 2:5 NKJV).

Perception can be a killer. Let me give some examples: Children can perceive that a teacher or parent doesn't like them when they are told no for their own good. Or a woman might perceive her husband isn't in love with her anymore because he's become comfortable and secure in their marriage and finds it okay to play video games instead of planning a date night.

In these examples, it's what the person *perceives* as truth that builds their belief system.

Perception is coming to a conclusion based on what we hear, see, or imagine. And it can be a killer to those who are insecure or who simply lack wisdom and knowledge. Other words that describe perception are awareness, observation, impression, or discernment. But the bottom line is that perception is individual.

In other words, every person controls their own perceptions, and their beliefs are fueled by what they allow in their thoughts and heart.

The Bible says Jesus often discerned the thoughts (or we could say, perceptions) of others. For example, after he fed the four thousand, He said to his disciples,

Take heed, beware of the leaven of the Pharisees and the leaven of Herod." And they reasoned among themselves, saying, "It is because we have no bread." But Jesus, being aware of it, said to them, "Why do you reason because you have no bread? Do you not yet perceive nor understand? Is your heart still hardened? Having eyes, do you not see? And having ears, do you not hear?"
(Mark 8:15–18 NKJV)

This is a perfect example to help us understand the dangers of perception. The disciples formed an opinion based on their lack of information (something people do every day). But their perception also revealed what they believed about Jesus: they thought He was mad at them. You see, when we fall short of putting God's word in our hearts, our perception will be full of distortions, lies, and compromises that only feel like the truth. And feelings (without truth) are dangerous.

Unfortunately, Job is operating in subjective perception too. He lacks a lot of information about his situation and the character of God. So, holding on to his feelings (and therefore, his resentment), Job continues his criticism of God,

I am disgusted with my life. Let me complain freely. My bitter soul must complain. I will say to God, 'Don't simply condemn me—tell me the charge you are bringing against me. What do you gain by oppressing me? Why do you reject me, the work of your own hands, while smiling on the schemes of the wicked? Are your eyes like those of a human? Do you see things only as people see them? Is your lifetime only as long as ours? Is your life so short that you must quickly probe for my guilt and search for my sin? Although you know I am not guilty, no one can rescue me from your hands. Yet your real motive—your true intent—was to watch me, and if I sinned, you would not forgive my guilt.

(10:1–7, 13–14)

Job originally didn't want to curse God but, sadly, he has forgotten about that. And here's a good question: Is criticizing God the same as cursing God? The answer leans toward yes because slandering one's character or using curse-styled words have the same effect. Slander is a defamation of character through malicious, false, and defamatory remarks— like cursing someone.

As Job's three friends listen to his ranting, although their view of God is tainted as well, they can't believe their friend would speak so harshly against God. Finally, Job's third friend speaks up.

> Then Zophar the Naamathite replied to Job: "Should I remain silent while you babble on? When you mock God, shouldn't someone make you ashamed? If only he would tell you the secrets of wisdom, for true wisdom is not a simple matter. Listen! God is doubtless punishing you far less than you deserve! If only you would prepare your heart and lift up your hands to him in prayer! Get rid of your sins and leave all iniquity behind you. Then your face will brighten in innocence. You will be strong and free of fear."
>
> (11:1, 3, 6, 13–15)

Zophar can't believe Job's enraged demeanor. He's in shock that such ugliness would come out of his friend's heart. If Zophar originally came to accuse Job of wrongdoing or sin, he has some proof now.

Uncontrolled Flesh

All of us struggle with the flesh because it has a voice. Paul said in Romans 7:23, "There is another power within me that is at war with my mind. This power makes me a slave to the sin that is still within me." He was talking about the urge to say or think something ugly. Paul understood that even when we know the right thing to say and do, there is always a contrary pull: our flesh. And when we yield to it, we become a slave to every one of its ugly emotions.

Job can't hear the warning of his friends. His anger and resentment mixed with his self-righteousness have given his flesh a driving force. Job presumes his own innocence and is completely unaware of his unrighteous behavior. He's even more unaware that in order for these things to come out of his mouth, they must first be in his heart.

> Then Job spoke again: "You people really know everything, don't you? And when you die, wisdom will die with you! Well, I know a few things myself—and you're no better than I am. Who doesn't know these things you've been saying? Just ask the animals, and they will teach you. Ask the birds of the sky, and they will tell you. Speak to the earth, and it will instruct you. Let the fish of the sea speak to you. For they all know that my disaster has come from the hand of the Lord. Yes, strength and wisdom are his; deceivers and deceived are both in his power."
>
> (12:1–3, 7–9, 16)

Job was oblivious to the fact he could be the deceived he's speaking of. And he still believed his works of righteousness were the only thing God desires.

God said Job was a blameless and upright man, but as already stated, he didn't say Job was perfect. This is where people have missed the core of this story. They want to make Job perfect and God right in allowing tragedy for no reason. But both of these thoughts contradict the rest of Bible.

What's not readily seen in the early part of this story is Job's belief that his works, his adherence to a godly life, are enough to protect him. This is what we all have in common with Job. Christians tend to think if they just go to church and follow the do's and don'ts of God's Word, then all should be good. But God requires us to keep our hearts in check as well. **Our inside motives matter more to God than our outward actions.** However, the two should work together. Ephesians 2:8-10 says our good works cannot produce righteousness, but righteousness (of the heart) should produce good works. And as we'll see in later chapters, Job had this backwards.

Not Godless

Look, I have seen all this with my own eyes and heard it with my own ears, and now I understand.

I know as much as you do. You are no better than I am. As for me, I would speak directly to the Almighty. I want to argue my case with God himself. As for you, you smear me with lies. As physicians, you are worthless quacks. Are you defending God with lies? Do you make your dishonest arguments for his sake?

Will you slant your testimony in his favor? Will you argue God's case for him? Be silent now and leave me alone. Let me speak—and I will face the consequences. Why should I put myself in mortal danger and take my life in my own hands? God might kill me, but I have no other hope. I am going to argue my case with him. But this is what will save me—I am not godless. If I were, I could not stand before him. Listen closely to what I am about to say. Hear me out. I have prepared my case; I will be proved innocent.

(13:1–4, 7–8, 13–18)

Job seemed to become slightly aware of his behavior, but he didn't care anymore. Either that or he was now hoping that what he believed about God was true and that at any moment, he would be put out of his misery when lightning struck him.

This is another example of Job criticizing God by criticizing his friends. This isn't in the form of "curse God!" but it is judgment toward God because he's accusing his friends of siding with God and not him (as if God could be wrong). Job was confident he has done nothing wrong. Yet the Bible says "if we say we have no sin [refusing to admit that we are sinners], we delude and lead ourselves astray, and the Truth [which the gospel presents] is not in us [does not dwell in our hearts]" (1 John 1:8, AMP).

Listen carefully: Job believed what would save him was that he was not "godless." The New King James says, "He also shall be my salvation, for a hypocrite could not come before Him" (Job 13:16). This statement that he wasn't "godless" or a hypocrite was another indicator of Job's true heart. And this is also what God had foreseen in him. Although God told Satan Job was a blameless and upright man, one who fears the Lord and abstains from evil, this didn't mean God was oblivious to the unstableness and misunderstandings of Job's heart.

Have you ever wondered why God allowed Satan to do so much evil to Job? It was not for punishment. God doesn't operate that way. God loved Job, just as he loves you and me. But James 1:26 warns, "If you claim to be religious but don't control your tongue, you are just fooling yourself, and your religion is worthless" (NLT). All of Job's faith-related actions—his strict ability to do what God required—deceived him into thinking he was better than he really was—thus moving him ever so slowly away from God and into Satan's hand.

Job had fooled himself. To say that he was not godless was almost the same as saying he was a god. This kind of religious thinking is worthless and an abomination to God Himself. And it's exactly what got Lucifer cast out of heaven. The New King James Version says, "For a hypocrite could not come before Him . . . " The Amplified Bible says, "a polluted and godless man shall not come before Him." The word *godless* here means to be profane, to pollute, or to corrupt. Job is boasting that he is none of those things, therefore he has every right to march into God's courtroom and demand an answer. But who of us in our right mind believes we could really do that? The Bible speaks of going boldly to the throne room of grace to find help, yes, but notice it's the throne room of "grace" not over-confidence, pride, or self-righteousness (Hebrews 4:16). This is why what Job was saying revealed how he thought and what's in his heart.

In the end, it's exactly what God asks him: "Who do you think you are?"

God loved Job, but He needed him to see how polluted his belief system had become. Job has shifted into believing that his works of righteousness were greater than God Himself. And in his deceived condition, Job just wants to vent. It is the way of our flesh to have the last word—right or wrong. It is an evil vortex that sucks us in and momentarily feels good.

Fortunately, if any good resides in our hearts, it will surface eventually. And as Job calmed down, he began to think clearly, and for the first time, he humbled himself and prayed,

> O God, grant me these two things, and then I will be able to face you. Remove your heavy hand from me, and don't terrify me with your awesome presence. Now summon me, and I will answer! Or let me speak to you, and you reply. Tell me, what have I done wrong? Show me my rebellion and my sin. Why do you turn away from me? Why do you treat me as your enemy?
>
> (13:20–24)

It's worth repeating: "Before destruction the heart of a man is haughty, *and before honor is humility*" (Proverbs 18:12, emphasis added).

CHAPTER FIVE
Read Job, Chapters 14-23

Boundaries and Controlling Factors

When we call on God from a pure and humble heart, He promises to respond. "When they call on me, I will answer; I will be with them in trouble. I will rescue them and honor them" (Psalm 91:15). Yet in our moment of surrender, who we've surrounded ourselves with is important. In the vulnerable state between being carnal or spiritual, the voice of others can easily sway us one way or the other. Job was still struggling. Part of him wanted to honor and trust God, and part of him wanted answers, which is understandable. But he's still confused on what he actually believed about God. He said, "My sins would be sealed in a pouch, and you would cover my guilt. But instead, as mountains fall and crumble, and as rocks fall from a cliff, as water wears away the stones, and floods wash away the soil, so you destroy people's hope" (Job 15:17-19).

If Job was beginning to soften toward God, that all changed when his friend Eliphaz decided he had more to say:

A wise man wouldn't answer with such empty talk!

You are nothing but a windbag. Have you no fear of God, no reverence for him? Your sins are telling your mouth what to say. Your words are based on clever deception. Your own mouth condemns you, not I. Your own lips testify against you. What has taken away your reason? What has weakened your vision, that you turn against God and say all these evil things? Can any mortal be pure? Can anyone born of a woman be just?

(15:2, 4–6, 12–14)

Eliphaz actually had some truth to what he was saying, but his haughty attitude only rekindled the dying fire in Job.

Overwhelmed

Then Job spoke again: I have heard all this before. What miserable comforters you are! Won't you ever stop blowing hot air? What makes you keep on talking? I could say the same things if you were in my place. I could spout off my criticism and shake my head at you. But if it were me, I would encourage you. I would try to take away your grief. Instead, I suffer if I defend myself, And I suffer no less if I refuse to speak.

(16:1–6)

Job was frustrated with his friends for their lack of understanding. He still believed he was innocent, but he was also understandably tired and overwhelmed.

O God, you have ground me down and devastated my family. As if to prove I have sinned, you've reduced me to skin and bones. My gaunt flesh testifies against me. God hates me and angrily tears me apart. He snaps his teeth at me and pierces me with his eyes. I was living quietly until he shattered me. He took me by the neck and broke me in pieces. Then he set me up as his target, and now his archers surround me. His arrows pierce me without mercy. The ground is wet with my blood. I wear burlap to show my grief. My pride lies in the dust. My eyes are red with weeping; dark shadows circle my eyes. Yet I have done no wrong, and my prayer is pure.

(16:7–9, 12-13, 15–17)

Job's view of God continued to have traces of dishonor. He believed God hated him and that God loved to kill whomever he chose, as if God was bored and needed target practice.

Job was teetering between a distorted view of God and his strong belief in his own innocence. Again, in desperation, he called on a mediator. "Even now my witness is in heaven. My advocate is there on high. My friends scorn me, but I pour out my tears to God. I need someone to mediate between God and me, as a person mediates between friends" (16:19-21).

As mentioned before, when sorting through our emotions, we often forget that faith and feelings are two different things. We weed through it all, rummaging for the truth, but in the process, we sometimes pull out all kinds of crazy and irrational thinking as well. Job asked for a mediator. He pleaded with God but continued to struggle with his feelings.

> You must defend my innocence, O God, since no one else will stand up for me. As for all of you, come back with a better argument, though I still won't find a wise man among you. My days are over. My hopes have disappeared. My heart's desires are broken. What if I call the grave my father, and the maggot my mother or my sister? Where then is my hope? Can anyone find it? No, my hope will go down with me to the grave. We will rest together in the dust!
> (17:3, 10–11, 14–16)

No Help at All

And no more than Job could keep his mouth quiet and his emotions in check, neither could his friends. They were bent on convincing him of his wrongdoing. Now Bildad got in on the act.

> How long before you stop talking? Speak sense if you want us to answer! Do you think we are mere animals? Do you think we are stupid? You may tear out

your hair in anger, but will that destroy the earth? Will it make the rocks tremble? Surely the light of the wicked will be snuffed out. The sparks of their fire will not glow. The homes of the wicked will burn down; burning sulfur rains on their houses. People in the west are appalled at their fate; people in the east are horrified. They will say, "This was the home of a wicked person, the place of one who rejected God."

(18:2–5, 15, 20–21)

Job's friends were not any more convinced of his innocence than he was of his guilt. They strongly believe Job's calamities must have been the result of sin and that his punishment was from God and therefore well deserved. Sadly, their own skewed theology created such a conclusion. It was becoming more evident that they don't know God's character either. It is also becoming obvious to Job what kind of friends he has—although a true friend is one who will tell you the truth, even if it's not what you want to hear. In this case, however, Job's friends were misguided in their idea of truth and were proving to be of little help to him. So he confronted them for their abuse.

How long will you torture me? How long will you try to crush me with your words? You have already insulted me ten times. You should be ashamed of treating me so badly. Even if I have sinned, that is my concern, not yours. You think you're better than I am, using my humiliation as evidence of my sin. But it is God who has wronged me. capturing me in his net.

(19:2–6)

My Redeemer Lives

Job was mistaken, of course. He believed God had wronged him. But God is God, and who are we to say He is wrong? When things in life appear unjustified, God invites us to ask for understanding and wisdom. But we must be careful not to arrive at conclusions before God has answered our prayer.

Despite all of Job's misguided notions, seeds of hope continued to surface occasionally. As he rebuked his friends, he boldly told them,

Must you persecute me, like God does? Haven't you chewed me up enough? Oh, that my words could be recorded. Oh, that they could be inscribed on a monument, carved with an iron chisel and filled with lead, engraved forever in the rock. But as for me, I know that my Redeemer lives, and he will stand upon the earth at last. And after my body has decayed, yet in my body I will see God! I will see him for myself. Yes, I will see him with my own eyes. I am overwhelmed at the thought! How dare you go on persecuting me, saying, "It's his own fault"? You should fear punishment yourselves, for your attitude deserves punishment. Then you will know that there is indeed a judgment.

(19:23–29)

Job believed his Redeemer lived. The word *redeemer* means to buy back from bondage, but remember this was long before God sent His Son Jesus to redeem mankind. Job's words were definitely prophetic, but in context here, in the middle of his situation, his call for a redeemer was still linked to the fact that he believed he was in undeserved bondage.

Job's glimmering ray of faith reminds me of a lesson I once learned. During a time when my husband and I were struggling financially (in our own sort of bondage), I went to the cabinet one evening to see what I could prepare for dinner. Other than staples like salt and flour, we had only a single can of ranch-style beans and some ground beef—and several more days before pay day. This wasn't the first time I'd seen a bare cupboard, but in that moment I was frustrated at the lying voice in my head that questioned God's faithfulness to His children. I realized right then and there I needed to decide what I believed.

As I looked at that can of beans, I loudly said, "Devil, this is a win-win situation. We will either eat this last can of beans, die, and go to heaven, or God will provide." It seems silly now, but I had to decide whether or not I was going to continue believing the devil's lies about God. So right there in my kitchen, I made my decision: *win-win.* Like Job, I believed my Redeemer lived, and this faith gave me the confidence to turn my accusations against the enemy instead of God.

Job also sees his situation as win-win, but for different reasons. He believes if he dies, he will be with God, and if he lives, he will be justified and proven right that he has been wronged. His real problem still lingers, however, because he so strongly believes in his own innocence that he's not willing to humble himself and examine his heart. His accusations are still towards God and not his real enemy.

Issues of the Heart

After enduring further put-downs from his friends, Job speaks again:

Listen closely to what I am saying. That's one consolation you can give me. Bear with me, and let me speak. After I have spoken, you may resume mocking me. My complaint is with God, not with people. I have good reason to be so impatient. Look at me and be stunned. Put your hand over your mouth in shock. When I think about what I am saying, I shudder. My body trembles. Why do the wicked prosper, growing old and powerful? They live to see their children grow up and settle down, and they enjoy their grandchildren. Their homes are safe from every fear, and God does not punish them. "Well," you say, "at least God will punish their children!" But I say he should punish the ones who sin, so that they understand his judgment. But who can teach a lesson to God, since he judges even the most powerful?

(21:1–9, 19, 22)

Is Job's haughtiness beginning to soften again? He is at least acknowledging the crazy way he's been talking. He says he knows God is just. He even acknowledges, "My complaint is with God..." Very slowly the truth is coming out, but Job's not ready to own any part of this yet or at least concede that the calamities that have come upon him might possibly be related to issues of his own heart.

Now's a good time to remind ourselves that there are many reasons Christians face adversities: persecution for righteousness (at the hand of Satan) or consequence of sin (discipline by God). If Job's trials were simply persecution for righteousness (in other words, for living a righteous life), God wouldn't have allowed Satan to touch him—this would go against God's own Word and nature. And this is why it's important to not read Job as a stand-alone book. Scripture is meant to interpret scripture. First Corinthians teaches us that the things recorded in the Old Testament are set forth as an example (10:6, NKJV). And the Bible says let all things be established by one or two witnesses (Matthew 18:16, NKJV), which means God's Word shouldn't contradict itself. Instead, it should establish itself by two or more references. So when we treat Job as a stand-alone book, we inadvertently create a stand-alone doctrine, and this mistake has kept countless people confused on God's true character.

To Job's protest, Eliphaz then replied:

Can a person do anything to help God? Can even a wise person be helpful to him? Is it any advantage to the Almighty if you are righteous? Would it be any gain to him if you were perfect? Is it because you're so pious that he accuses you and brings judgment against you? No, it's because of your wickedness! There's no limit to your sins. If you return to the Almighty, you will be restored—so clean up your life. If you give up your lust for money and throw your precious gold into the river, the Almighty himself will be your treasure. He will be your precious silver! Then you will take delight in the Almighty and look up to God. You will pray to him, and he will hear you, and you will fulfill your vows to him.

(22:2–5, 23–27)

Here again truth is mixed with deception. Eliphaz is being sarcastic to Job. He hears Job's claims of innocence and mocks him by saying, "Is it because of your reverence for God that he accuses and judges you?" Job's friends strongly believe that God must be punishing him for something, but they haven't been able to prove it yet. Eliphaz just presumes Job deserves this treatment, so he throws out a mention of riches and wealth. After all, Job had been the richest man around. Yet the real reason Eliphaz, Bildad, and Zophar cannot pinpoint Job's sin is because it's an issue of the heart, one with which they too are contaminated.

Separation

Then Job spoke again:

My complaint today is still a bitter one, and I try hard not to groan aloud. If only I knew where to find God, I would go to his court. I would lay out my case and present my arguments. Then I would listen to his reply and understand what he says to me. I go east, but he is not there. I go west, but I cannot find him. I do not see him in the north, for he is hidden. I look to the south, but he is concealed.

(23:1–4, 8–9)

Sin separates us from God. The Bible clearly says He will never leave us nor forsake us, but we however, can forsake God by building walls within us that keep Him at a distance. When Job says he can't find God, it's not because God has left him.

All sin, including pride and self-righteousness, separate us from God. And whether it's knowingly or unknowingly, our misgivings toward sin don't move God—we're the ones who move, not Him. Sometimes we can't see or feel God's presence because of the walls that separate us, but this doesn't mean we are left alone. God was never far from Job during his entire ordeal.

What Can I Do?

Job continues his argument, saying,

But he knows where I am going. And when he tests me, I will come out as pure as gold. For I have stayed on God's paths; I have followed his ways and not

turned aside. I have not departed from his commands
but have treasured his words more than daily food.

(23:10–12)

As the old cliché reminds us, sometimes we can't see the forest for the trees. Job was still blinded to the fact that his works could never be enough to make him right with God. Remember the rich young ruler who approached Jesus? He, too, thought his works would be sufficient:

Now a certain ruler asked [Jesus], saying, "Good Teacher, what shall I do to inherit eternal life?" So Jesus said to him, "Why do you call Me good? No one is good but One, that is, God. You know the commandments: *'do not commit adultery,' 'do not murder,' 'do not steal,' 'do not bear false witness,' 'honor your father and your mother.'"* And [the ruler] said, "All these things I have kept from my youth."

(Luke 18:18–21, NKJV)

The ruler seemed to have been sincere in asking Jesus how to find eternal life. But notice that he asked Jesus what he could *do.* Like Job, he thought his works could be sufficient to earn him right-standing with God, but "Salvation is not a reward for the good things we have done, so none of us can boast about it" (Ephesians 2:9). When Jesus "heard these things, he said to [the ruler], 'You still lack one thing. Sell all that you have and distribute to the poor, and you will have treasure in heaven; and come, follow Me.' But when he heard this, he became very sorrowful, for he was very rich" (Luke 18:22–23). Jesus gave the young ruler another "do" instruction to reveal what his heart really contained. Jesus often did this. He would give an instruction to locate the person's belief system. In this case, the ruler sincerely approached Jesus but mentioned all the things he had done obviously believing these were the things God was looking for. Yet again, this is why self-righteousness is so deceiving—there's nothing in "self" that can make us right with God. Our first approach must be based on faith and trust, and then followed by good actions. The ruler didn't trust Jesus could be better for him than his wealth, so therefore, he couldn't "do" what was asked. This was first a heart condition that resulted in an action (or inaction in this case).

God knows every heart, just as Jesus already knew the young ruler struggled with an attachment to his possessions more than he should and had more trust in his righteous duties than in God. Likewise, Job had been careful to follow what he believed honored God in outward action and religious duty. But without realizing it, he had developed a greater trust in his ability to do these things than in any righteousness (favor and approval) that comes from God through faith.

Proverbs 16:2 says, "Humans are satisfied with whatever looks good; God probes for what is good" (MSG).

CHAPTER SIX
Read Job, Chapters 24-27

The Double-Minded Man

When people don't understand situations and circumstances from a natural point of view, it is not uncommon to hear someone say, "Well, God is sovereign. He can do what He wants." But let's clarify sovereignty. It is defined as God's absolute right to do all things according to His own good pleasure. But this concept has been misunderstood by man from the beginning of time because it doesn't mean everything that happens is the will of God. God is first and foremost sovereign to His Word, meaning, God's will is always found in God's Word. He won't lie, and He doesn't contradict Himself (even if people don't have a full knowledge or understand of His decisions or methods).

The Bible says, "For just as the heavens are higher than the earth, so my ways are higher than your ways and my thoughts higher than your thoughts [says the Lord]" (Isaiah 55:9, paraphrase added). God gave us His Word to give us guidelines. And

God's Word is God's law. Paul said in Romans 4:15, "Where there is no law there is no transgression" (NKJV). In other words, the only way to avoid breaking the law is to have no law to break.

So the law (God's Word) was, and is, necessary, but it was *never* intended to be greater than the Lawmaker.

The Humble Will Be Honored

In Luke 18, we find an account that might help us to better understand this principle:

> Then Jesus told this story to some who had great confidence in their own righteousness and scorned everyone else: "Two men went to the Temple to pray. One was a Pharisee, and the other was a despised tax collector. The Pharisee stood by himself and prayed this prayer: 'I thank you, God, that I am not like other people—cheaters, sinners, adulterers. I'm certainly not like that tax collector! I fast twice a week, and I give you a tenth of my income.' But the tax collector stood at a distance and dared not even lift his eyes to heaven as he prayed. Instead, he beat his chest in sorrow, saying, 'O God, be merciful to me, for I am a sinner.' I tell you, this sinner, not the Pharisee, returned home justified before God. For those who exalt themselves will be humbled, and those who humble themselves will be exalted."
>
> (Luke 18: 9–14)

The Pharisee had made his obedience to follow God's written law greater than God Himself. But the tax collector did just the opposite. He acknowledged his sin and humbled himself before God. In our own lives, there should always be a balance between following God's commands (which are intended for our well-being) and recognizing that none of us are without sin, no matter how well we follow what He has told us.

Sin is disobedience to God's commands, so the Pharisee thought he was without sin because he had obeyed. But remember, deception is reality minus the truth. The reality was that he had followed the logistics of the law. The truth was he had slipped over into arrogance and self-confidence. This defied God's moral law and therefore produced sin. Exodus 20:3 says, "You shall have no other gods before Me" (NKJV). This would include making our obedience a god.

Good or Bad?

The main emphasis of this book is to enlighten us on the importance God places on the heart of man versus the actions of man. And in turn, how this determines our view of God.

God will judge us all by the intent of our hearts followed by the actions that resulted from such.

Therefore, there's no argument Job was faithful in his obedience to God's commands, but what he didn't realize was that he was guilty of making his obedience greater than God. And in so doing, Job began to judge God:

Why doesn't the Almighty bring the wicked to judgment? Why must the godly wait for him in vain? Evil people steal land by moving the boundary markers. They steal livestock and put them in their own pastures. They even take the orphan's donkey and demand the widow's ox as security for a loan. The poor must go about naked, without any clothing. They harvest for others while they themselves are starving. They press out olive oil without being allowed to taste it, and they tread in the winepress as they suffer from thirst. The groans of the dying rise from the city, and the wounded cry for help, yet God ignores their moaning.

(24:1–3, 10–12)

Job believed God was sovereign, but he seemed to think this meant everything that happened was the will of God. This isn't true.

In fact, to believe in the goodness of God, we must also acknowledge the enemies of God. Job has failed to do this. And remember, just because Job accused God does not mean that what he was saying is true. In his anger and frustration, Job charged God with being deaf to the poor, yet he believed that God did and will punish the ungodly. Job seemed to contradict himself here. One statement makes God look bad, and the other makes Him look good. So which is it?

Job continues:

The grave consumes sinners just as drought and heat consume snow. Their own mother will forget him. Maggots will find them sweet to eat. No one will remember him. Wicked people are broken like a tree in the storm. God, in his power, drags away the rich. They may rise high, but they have no assurance in life. They may be allowed to live in security, but God is always watching them. And though they are great now, in a moment they will be gone like all others, cut off like heads of grain. Can anyone claim otherwise? Who can prove me wrong?

(24:19–20, 22–25)

It seems that no one would be able to convince Job. He ranted about the fate of sinners but he saw no parallel between what he was saying and his own circumstances. You would think if he so strongly believed this, he would have at least paused and asked God, "Where did I miss it? Let me repent if I did..."

God's Justice

In Ezekiel, God told the prophet to explain His divine justice.

"There's more, son of man. Tell your people, 'A good person's good life won't save him when he decides to rebel, and a bad person's bad life won't prevent him from repenting of his rebellion. A good person who sins can't expect to live when he chooses to sin. It's true that I tell good people, "Live! Be alive!" But if they trust in their good deeds and turn to evil, that good life won't amount to a hill of beans. They'll die for their evil life. 'On the other hand, if I tell a wicked person, "You'll die for your wicked life," and he repents of his sin and starts living a righteous and just life—being generous to the down-and-out, restoring what he had stolen, cultivating life-nourishing ways that don't hurt others—he'll live. He won't die. None of his sins will be kept on the books. He's doing what's right, living a good life. He'll live. Your people say, "The Master's way isn't fair." But it's the way *they're* living that isn't fair. When good people turn back from living good lives and plunge into sin, they'll die for it. And when a wicked person turns away from his wicked life and starts living a just and righteous life, he'll come alive.

(Ezekiel 33:12–19, MSG)

God is not unfair. The past actions of righteousness cannot save someone if he forsakes right living and turns to sin any more than past sins can condemn a person who forsakes them and repents.

Job boldly claimed God was unjust. His friends, on the other hand, believed God was distant and remote and should be feared. Listen to what Bildad came up with:

God is powerful and dreadful. He enforces peace in the heavens. Who is able to count his heavenly army? Doesn't his light shine on all the earth? How can a mortal be innocent before God? Can anyone born of a woman be pure? God is more glorious than the moon; he shines brighter than the stars. In comparison, people are maggots; we mortals are mere worms.

(25:2–6)

Both Job and his friends were operating in a mixture of truth and deception. Job was wrong: *God is a just God*—He's not unfair. Yet his friends were wrong too: *God is a loving God*—He is not dreadful and has no desire to squash us like bugs. His people are precious to him. As the saying goes, "God loves the sinner, not the sin."

Conflicting Beliefs

Bildad's speech doesn't satisfy Job. He retorts:

How you have helped the powerless! How you have saved the weak! How you have enlightened my stupidity! What wise advice you have offered! Where have you gotten all these wise sayings? Whose spirit speaks through you? God stretches the northern sky over empty space and hangs the earth on nothing. He wraps the rain in his thick clouds, and the clouds don't burst with the weight. He covers the face of the moon, shrouding it with his clouds. He created the horizon when he separated the waters; he set the boundary between day and night. These are just the beginning of all that he does, merely a whisper of his power. Who, then, can comprehend the thunder of his power?

(26:1–4, 7–10, 14)

Job had no argument against God's supremacy. But because he was so frustrated with his friends' lack of understanding for his situation, he used sarcasm in his depiction of God's enormous power.

It's important to understand there are sins more dangerous than the outward, visible, obvious sins such as murder, adultery, and so on (all of which are bad of course). In fact, the majority of outward sins are a result of sins of the heart that are never dealt with. So the real danger is in not recognizing or dealing with things that creep into our heart long before these outward evidences appear. In ministry, I have counseled people for over 20 years, and in every case, there were issues of the heart that existed long before the outward sins and problems appeared. And most of these issues of the heart stemmed from a wrong mindset that had been fueled by deception and lies of the enemy because the person didn't know God's truth.

The story of Job highlights issues that we all face. Therefore, it's the perfect illustration of God's love and mercy because as we'll soon find out when Job is confronted, God cares about the issues of the heart. But for now, Job isn't budging on his belief that a person's religious duty is more important than what he thinks or says.

> I vowed by the living God, who has taken away my rights, by the Almighty who has embittered my soul— As long as I live, while I have breath from God, my lips will speak no evil, and my tongue will speak no lies. I will never concede that you are right; I will defend my integrity until I die. I will maintain my innocence without wavering. My conscience is clear for as long as I live. For what hope do the godless have when God cuts them off and takes away their life? Will God listen to their cry when trouble comes upon them? Can they take delight in the Almighty? Can they call to God at any time? I will teach you about God's power. I will not conceal anything that concerns the Almighty. But you have seen all this, yet you say all these useless things to me.
>
> (27:2–6, 8–12)

My conscious is never 100% percent clear. Is yours? The more I learn God's Word, the more I borrow David's prayer: "May the words of my mouth and the meditation of my heart be pleasing to you, O Lord, my rock and my redeemer" (Psalm 19:14). In other words, "Check me God." I know I'm human and therefore prone to some error. We can have confidence in

God, but we need to be careful of having too much confidence in ourselves.

Paul said in Romans 9:31–32, "The people of Israel, who tried so hard to get right with God by keeping the law, never succeeded. Why not? Because they were trying to get right with God by keeping the law instead of by trusting in him. They stumbled over the great rock in their path." Poor Job was stumbling all over the place. He was determined to maintain his innocence. "My righteousness I hold fast, and will not let it go; my heart shall not reproach me as long as I live" (27:6 NKJV). Sadly however, Job didn't realize he was teetering on the line of deceptive persuasion. Satan thought he was right too.

In fact, Satan thought he was greater than God. "For you have said in your heart: 'I will ascend into heaven, I will exalt my throne above the stars of God; I will also sit on the mount of the congregation on the farthest sides of the north; I will ascend above the heights of the clouds, I will be like the Most High'" (Isaiah 14:13–14 NKJV).

Job hadn't gone this far. He hadn't said he wanted to be like God, but by holding on to *his* righteousness, he was foolishly claiming to be more than he really was. "Shall the potter be esteemed as the clay? Shall the thing made say of him who made it, 'He did not make me?' Or shall the thing formed say of him who formed it, 'He has no understanding'?" (Isaiah 29:16, NKJV).

CHAPTER SEVEN

Read Job, Chapters 24-27

Spiritual Insanity

Proverbs 13:10 says, "Pride leads to conflict..." so is it any wonder Job and his three friends are locked in strife? Strife is the manifest presence of the devil, and peace is the manifest presence of God. Satan is proud, and all who operate in pride are operating under his influence. "For all that is in the world—the lust of the flesh, the lust of the eyes, and the pride of life—is not of the Father but is of the world" (1 John 2:16, NKJV).

Good Job . . . Well Done

Besides strife, another side-effect of pride is spiritual insanity. Pride causes us to lose all good sense, wisdom, reason, and understanding. Pride tempts people to lift themselves higher than God himself, forgetting who He is or what He has done for them. But the real insanity is that pride doesn't realize it is tethered to bondage and has only risen higher in its own mind.

The danger of this kind of pride can be seen in Daniel 4 regarding the great kingdom established under King Nebuchadnezzar's rule. God greatly blessed him with riches and power, yet he fell into the trap of thinking his great wealth had come by his own hand. He patted himself on the back and said, "Good job. Well done."

> As he looked out across the city, he said, "Look at this great city of Babylon! By my own mighty power, I have built this beautiful city as my royal residence to display my majestic splendor."
>
> (Daniel 4:30)

By giving himself the credit for his success, King Nebuchadnezzar fell into pride and took all the glory away from God. But not for long.

A Dose of Humility

"While these words were still in his mouth, a voice called down from heaven, 'O King Nebuchadnezzar, this message is for you! You are no longer ruler of this kingdom'" (4:31). Because of his pride, the kingdom God had made Nebuchadnezzar steward over was stripped from him and he was cast down. And this is the danger when things are going well. Satan will whisper thoughts of "I" and "my" in our heads. And if we listen and begin meditating on those thoughts, we may find ourselves operating in pride too. Satan has always wanted God's glory. Remember, it was pride that caused him to be cast down in the first place.

But a humble heart will be lifted up. "After this time had passed, I, Nebuchadnezzar, looked up to heaven. My sanity returned, and I praised and worshiped the Most High and honored the one who lives forever. His rule is everlasting, and his kingdom is eternal. Now I, Nebuchadnezzar, praise and glorify and honor the King of heaven. All his acts are just and true, and he is able to humble the proud" (4:34, 37).

King Nebuchadnezzar said his "sanity" returned. He acknowledged that it goes against all good sense to think that we can take credit for any successes in life. Proverbs 11:2 says, "Pride leads to disgrace, but with humility comes wisdom." Sadly, we sometimes have to be humbled in order to open our eyes so we can see clearly and operate in true wisdom.

I, My, and Me

Unlike Nebuchadnezzar, Job's pride stemmed from his works, not his wealth. But in either case, both were guilty of patting themselves on the back. Job wasn't operating in true wisdom yet, but he had been humbled. If only pride would step out of the way so wisdom could come forth. Let's listen to what he said next.

I long for the years gone by when God took care of me, when he lit up the way before me and I walked safely through the darkness. Those were the days when

I went to the city gate and took my place among the honored leaders. The young stepped aside when they saw me, and even the aged rose in respect at my coming. The princes stood in silence and put their hands over their mouths. The highest officials of the city stood quietly, holding their tongues in respect. All who heard me praised me. All who saw me spoke well of me. Everything I did was honest. Righteousness covered me like a robe, and I wore justice like a turban. Everyone listened to my advice. They were silent as they waited for me to speak. And after I spoke, they had nothing to add, for my counsel satisfied them.

(29:2–3, 7-11, 14, 21–22)

Reread this paragraph, and count how many times Job used the words "I" and "my" and "me." He said he longed for the days when God was with him, but it's only a mention of God—he never really gives Him credit for His wisdom or affluence. And although at first glance it may appear this mention of God is meant to honor Him, Job's following statements refuted that thinking when his haughtiness showed up in grand style as he judged the young men whose fathers ". . . are not worthy to run with my sheepdogs" (Job 30:1). We can certainly give Job some grace because of his situation, but it's impossible to ignore the pride and judgmental attitude that must have been in his heart long before he ever spoke it aloud.

Daniel 2:20 (NKJV) says, "Blessed be the name of God forever and ever, for wisdom and might are His." Any wisdom we have obtained comes from God. In fact, Proverbs 2:6 tells us, "The Lord gives wisdom; from His mouth come knowledge and understanding" (NKJV).

Earlier, it appeared Job understood God's sovereignty, acknowledging He was the source of all wisdom. He asks,

> Do people know where to find wisdom? Where can they find understanding? No one knows where to find it, for it is not found among the living. "It is not here," says the ocean. "Nor is it here," says the sea. It cannot be bought with gold It cannot be purchased with silver. God alone understands the way to wisdom; he knows where it can be found, for he looks throughout the whole earth and sees everything under the heavens. And this is what he says to all humanity: "The fear of the Lord is true wisdom; to forsake evil is real understanding."
>
> (28:6, 12–15, 23-24, 28)

It sounds here as if Job comprehended that all wisdom was from God, but it was immediately *after* these statements that he began to reminisce about his glory days—giving himself all the credit. So in light of everything, it appears Job believed that people who feared the Lord (or in this case, people who were afraid of breaking God's commands), were the only ones who had any wisdom. And there is some truth to that, but in context, Job was patting himself on the back for "fearing" God while never actually giving Him any recognition. Is that wisdom?

Job had repeatedly insisted on his innocence, pointing out to his friends how he hadn't disobeyed or dishonored God in any way, but then failed to realize he had abandoned all good sense by wishing for the days when *he* was an important person in the city gates—when *his* wisdom was honored.

Filthy Rags

Job's double-mindedness was obvious. At times he appeared to be coming to his senses, returning from spiritual insanity or pride, only to return to it later. Job's main care right now was his reputation.

But now I am mocked by those who are younger than I,
by young men whose fathers are not worthy to run with
my sheepdogs. They despise me and won't come near me,
except to spit in my face. For God has cut my bowstring.
He has humbled me, so they have thrown off all restraint.

(30:1, 10–11)

His words were arrogant and self-inflated. He mentioned that it was God who is humbling him, and yet he didn't see why. This is what pride does: it blinds us. And in Job's blindness, he thought he was wearing garments of honor and esteem, and that all who looked upon him could see his great worth. But the proud man in his blindness cannot see that he, like the homeless man in my early parable of the barber, is dirty, unshaven, and a mess. "We are all infected and impure with sin. When we proudly display our righteous deeds, we find they are nothing but filthy rags" (Isaiah 64:6).

Self-justification is a person's vain attempt to find restoration with God through personal merit. Job was a good man, but his pride had led to foolish talking and his insistent stand that he should be justified. Matthew 12:36–37 warns that "for every idle word men may speak, they will give account of it in the day of judgment. For by your words you will be justified, and by your words you will be condemned" (NKJV). Job was blameless in following his prescribed set of laws, but this fact only fuels his adamancy he's innocent.

I cry to you, O God, but you don't answer. I stand before you, and you don't even look. You have become cruel toward me. You use your power to persecute me. Did I not weep for those in trouble? Was I not deeply grieved for the needy?... I made a covenant with my eyes not to look with lust upon a young woman... Have I lied to anyone or deceived anyone?... If I have been unfair to my male or female servants when they brought their complaints to me, how could I face God? What could I say when he questioned me? For God created both me and my servants. He created us both in the womb... Have I put my trust in money or felt secure because of my gold?... If so, I should be punished by the judges, for it would mean I had denied the God of heaven. Have I ever rejoiced when disaster struck my enemies, or become excited when harm came their way? No, I have never sinned by cursing anyone or by asking for revenge. If only someone would listen to me! Look, I will sign my name to my defense. Let the Almighty answer me. Let my accuser write out the charges against me.

(30:20–21, 25;)

(31:1, 5, 13–15, 24, 28–30, 35)

Without Sin

Self-justification is a deceptive sin. "For there is not a just man on earth who does good and does not sin" (Ecclesiastes 7:20 NKJV). Job's eyes were so blinded. As he listed his good deeds, it was evident he believed he was without sin. But his sin was not that of breaking the law; his sin was his belief that he was without sin. And this belief somehow crept into his heart long before he ever spoke it.

At the beginning, God said Job was blameless and upright, but these words are not meant to be defined as "perfect." Blameless describes his works. Upright describes his intent. Job's intent was to honor and love God and he showed this through his works. But think about this: the placement of Job's story in the Bible was meant to help the thousands of us who would follow. What we learn here is that we can have good intentions yet ignore the warnings of pride and self-righteousness, which open a door for the enemy to take advantage of us.

Job wasn't a Pharisee, but pride and self-righteousness were much of what Jesus condemned in the Pharisees: "For I say to you, that unless your righteousness exceeds the righteousness of the scribes and Pharisees, you will by no means enter the kingdom of heaven" (Matthew 5:20, NKJV). And this is why Job's story will help us all. We need to be warned.

So it's important to remember that once we open our mouth, we are in danger, because unless we can bridle our tongues, none of us are able to remain blameless.

Indeed, we all make many mistakes. For if we could control our tongues, we would be perfect and could also control ourselves in every other way. We can make a large horse go wherever we want by means of a small bit in its mouth. And a small rudder makes a huge ship turn wherever the pilot chooses to go, even though the winds are strong. In the same way, the tongue is a small thing that makes grand speeches. But a tiny spark can set a great forest on fire. And among all the parts of the body, the tongue is a flame of fire. It is a whole world of wickedness, corrupting your entire body. It can set your whole life on fire, for it is set on fire by hell itself. People can tame all kinds of animals, birds, reptiles, and fish, but no one can tame the tongue. It is restless and evil, full of deadly poison. Sometimes it praises our Lord and Father, and sometimes it curses those who have been made in the image of God. And so blessing and cursing come pouring out of the same mouth. Surely, my brothers and sisters, this is not right!

(James 3:2–10)

No matter what form sin takes, the bottom line is that "all have sinned and fall short of the glory of God" (Romans 3:23, NKJV). Job is not alone. The flawed condition of humanity is exemplified in the best of men. Abraham lied about Sarah being his sister. Moses didn't trust God to demonstrate his holiness to the people and was not allowed to enter the promised land. Jehoshaphat was a good king, but he failed to remove all the pagan shrines in his kingdom. Jonah disobeyed by running from God. Even King David could not claim to be free of sin.

Since human imperfections keep us in sin, what can we do? Recognition of this truth is the first step. For example, the Scriptures say David was a man after God's own heart, although he was later found to be a murderer and an adulterer. Samuel said this of David when he announced the end of King Saul's reign (1 Samuel 13:14). So before David had even become king, God knew what was in his heart. He knew King David would fall into sin, but he also knew he would repent. And this is a large part of what made him a man after God's heart. It wasn't that David was without sin; it was that he could admit "against You [God], You only, have I sinned..." (Psalm 51:4, NKJV). This also helps us understand why God could say Job was blameless and upright in the beginning yet discover through his story that not all was right.

And when Job sees this about himself, he too will find help from God.

Nothing Left to Say

Job's life literally changed overnight. He was enjoying prosperity in every area when Satan attacked him. It must have been devastating to lose his entire family and all of his property. Then to be harmed physically as well must have been too much to bear. In our most faith-filled moments, many of us have cried out in our heart, "Lord, I love you! I'll serve you always! I'll never forsake you!" But if we were put in Job's shoes, could we maintain this? I don't know for sure, but I am certain that in such a time our hearts would be revealed, just as Job's had been.

What I would hope for in a situation like Job's is that my closest friends would be those who would tell me the truth because *they* know the Truth. Eliphaz, Bildad, and Zophar may have been Job's friends, but they were unable to help him. If only they had known what the psalmist did when he said God is "full of compassion, and gracious, longsuffering and abundant in mercy and truth" (Psalm 86:15, NKJV), then maybe they could have encouraged Job and opened his eyes. But they had a flawed view of God's character as well. Therefore they "refused to reply further to him because he kept insisting on his innocence" (Job 32:1).

CHAPTER EIGHT

Read Job, Chapters 32-35

The Bystander Speaks

At this point in our story, it seems Job and his friends were deadlocked. All were operating in measures of deception, yet each of them maintained their position, refusing to budge. Job had been unable to convince them of his innocence any more than they had been able to convince him of his guilt. The problem lied in their misconceptions about God.

During all of their rantings back and forth, a quiet bystander had been listening in:

"Then Elihu, son of Barakel the Buzite, from the clan of Ram, became very angry. He was angry because Job "justified himself rather than God" (32:2, NKJV). The <u>Amplified Bible</u> says Elihu's "indignation was kindled and burned and he became upset with Job because he justified himself rather than God [even expressed doubts about God's character]." And this explains why Elihu "was also angry with Job's three friends, for they made God appear to be wrong by their inability to answer Job's arguments" (Job 32:3).

Finally! We have someone who has understanding! Elihu's righteous anger is already an indicator that he must have had a different take on God. Proverbs 29:13 says, "The poor and the oppressor have this in common—the LORD gives light to the eyes of both" (NKJV). God is not in hiding. He will always reveal Himself to those who seek him. "And you will seek Me and find Me, when you search for Me with all your heart" (Jeremiah 29:13, NKJV). The problem with most people is they have believed the traditions of men (their parents, their pastors, their churches) without getting into the Scriptures for themselves. But God has promised that if we seek wisdom, we will find it. "I searched everywhere, determined to find wisdom and to understand the reason for things. I was determined to prove to myself that wickedness is stupid and that foolishness is madness" (Ecclesiastes 7:25).

Elihu was a man who sought after wisdom.

Elihu had waited for the others to speak because they were older than he. But when he saw that they had no further reply, he spoke out angrily. "I am young and you are old, so I held back from telling you what I think. I thought, 'Those who are older should speak, for wisdom comes with age.'... I have waited all this time, listening very carefully to your arguments, listening to you grope for words... Listen to my words Job, pay attention to what I have to say... Answer me, if you can; make your

case and take your stand... You have spoken in my hearing. and I have heard your very words. You said, 'I am
pure; I am without sin; I am innocent; I have no guilt.
God is picking a quarrel with me, and he considers me
his enemy. He puts my feet in the stocks and watches my every move.' But you are wrong, and I will show
you why. For God is greater than any human being."

$$(32:4-7, 11;)$$
$$(33:1, 5, 8-12)$$

Elihu openly acknowledged he was younger than Job and
his friends. Out of respect he had been silent. But we need to
understand that spiritual maturity has nothing to do with phys-
ical age. Spiritual maturity is not based on the number of years
you have been saved (or in this case, followed a set of rules or
performed religious duties without fail). Spiritual maturity is
based on our application of God's pure Word and our pursuit of
truth and wisdom. This is what keeps us humble, whereas just
following God's laws (in deed and not in heart) puts people too
close to the edge of pride and self-righteousness.

Breaking the Silence

Elihu had some understanding that Job and his three friends
did not. The more he sat and listened, the more indignant he
became. Indignation can be anger aroused by something unjust
or unworthy. And remember, *silence can be agreement*. Elihu

has now decided it was time to break his silence and speak up. He continued talking to Job:

"If an angel from heaven appears—a special messenger to intercede for a person and declare that he is upright—he will be gracious and say, 'Rescue him from the grave, for I have found a ransom for his life.' When he prays to God, he will be accepted. And God will receive him with joy and restore him to good standing. He will declare to his friends, 'I sinned, and I twisted the truth, but it was not worth it. God rescued me from the grave, and now my life is filled with light.' Yes, God often does these things again and again for people. He rescues them from the grave so they may enjoy the light of life. Mark this well, Job. Listen to me, for I have more to say. But if you have anything to say, go ahead. Speak, for I am anxious to see you justified. But if not, then listen to me. Keep silent and I will teach you wisdom!

(33:23–24, 26–33)

Job wished there was a mediator between him and God. And Elihu spoke of a mediator, stating that God would gladly make the exchange—a ransom—for our sins. But notice Elihu said, "When he prays to God, he will be accepted." This is a picture of a penitent heart, which knows no one is completely without sin. Elihu said, "Keep silent and I will teach you wisdom..." which could be interpreted as self-righteousness on Elihu's part, but later when God shows up and corrects Job and his friends, He doesn't correct Elihu at all. This is a very important piece of the story that too many people have overlooked.

If Elihu himself were in pride and self-righteousness, God would've thrown him into the bunch with the rest. But as we soon see, God allows Elihu to defend Him and set the record straight about how we are to approach and view God.

Tailored Justice

Elihu challenged Job to speak up and justify himself or keep quiet and listen. Elihu had Job's attention. Recognizing this, he turned his words toward all four men.

Listen to me, you wise men. Pay attention, you who have knowledge. Job said, 'The ear tests the words it hears just as the mouth distinguishes between foods.' So let us discern for ourselves what is right; let us learn together what is good. For Job has said, "I am innocent, but God has taken away my rights. I am innocent, but they call me a liar. My suffering is incurable, though I have not sinned." Tell me, has there ever been a man like Job, with his thirst for irreverent talk?... He has even said, 'Why waste time trying to please God?" Listen to me, you who have understanding. Everyone knows that God doesn't sin! The Almighty can do no wrong. He repays people according to their deeds. He treats people as they deserve. Truly, God will not do wrong. The Almighty will not twist justice. Did someone put the world in his care? Who set the whole world in place? If God were to take back his spirit and withdraw his breath, all life would cease, and humanity would turn again to dust. We don't set the time when we will come before God in judgment. He brings the mighty to ruin without asking anyone, and he sets up others in their place. He watches what they do, and in the night he overturns and destroys them. He strikes them down because they are wicked, doing it openly for all to see. For they have turned from following him. They have no respect for any of his ways.

(34:2–7, 9–15, 23–27)

I can almost picture Eliphaz, Bildad, and Zophar nodding their heads in agreement, saying "Yeah! Right!" Isn't this what they'd been trying to say all along?—that God destroys the wicked? Elihu agreed God was just. He knew God "shall judge the world in righteousness, and He shall administer judgment for the peoples in uprightness" (Psalm 9:8, NKJV). In context of God's divine justice, the New Living Translation may help us to better understand this verse: "He will judge the world with justice and rule the nations with fairness." You can be sure God will be fair. But Eliphaz, Bildad, and Zophar, in their quest for judgment, seemed to be ignorant of God's mercy.

Elihu knew what they were thinking, so he said, "Why don't people say to God, 'I have sinned, but I will sin no more'? Or 'I don't know what evil I have done—tell me. If I have done wrong, I will stop at once'? Must God tailor his justice to your demands?" (Job 34:31–33a). God is impartial. He will judge the righteous and the wicked, but He will show mercy to both as well. He is looking for a teachable spirit. But when we begin to judge God and think we know how He should handle affairs, then we have lost our ability to be taught. "God has chosen the foolish things of the world to put to shame the wise, and God has chosen the weak things of the world to put to shame the things which are mighty" (1 Corinthians 1:27, NKJV).

Not Finished Defending God

Just as Elihu was angry with Eliphaz, Bildad, and Zophar because they believed only in God's judgment and not his mercy, he was also angry with Job because he thought he was more righteous than God.

But you have rejected him! The choice is yours, not mine. Go ahead, share your wisdom with us. After all, bright people will tell me, and wise people will hear me say, 'Job speaks out of ignorance; his words lack insight.' Job, you deserve the maximum penalty for the wicked way you have talked. For you have added rebellion to your sin; you show no respect, and you speak many angry words against God... Do you think it is right for you to claim, 'I am righteous before God'? Yet you also ask, 'What's in it for me? What's the use of living a righteous life?' I will answer you and all your friends, too... If you sin, how does that affect God? Even if you sin again and again, what effect will it have on him? If you are good, is this some great gift to him? What could you possibly give him? No, your sins affect only people like yourself, and your good deeds also affect only humans.

(34:33b–37; 35:2–4, 6–8)

Elihu was boldly challenging all of their beliefs. He confronted Job by asking what benefit is it to God if you do good? And yet he's also challenged Job's friends by asking them what harm is it to God if you sin? In either case, the blessing or detriment is for us, not God. "But it is wrong to say God doesn't listen, to say the Almighty isn't concerned" (Job 35:13).

We are God's creation, and He very much cares about us. He gave us His Word to help us. God is not a big ogre sitting up in heaven waiting to strike us down when we disobey. But because He is just, then in time, justice will prevail. "The Lord is not slack concerning His promise, as some count slackness, but is longsuffering toward us, not willing that any should perish but that all should come to repentance" (2 Peter 3:9, NKJV).

"Elihu continued speaking: 'Let me go on, and I will show you the truth. **For I have not finished defending God!** I will present profound arguments for the righteousness of my Creator'" (36:1–3, emphasis added). Elihu was dauntless in his argument against Job and his companions. He was determined to set the record straight. He boldly declared, "I will fetch my knowledge from afar; I will ascribe righteousness to my Maker" (NKJV).

CHAPTER NINE

Read Job, Chapters 36-40

Understanding

R ighteousness is a big Bible word with even bigger bene-
fits. Under the new covenant, it is the gift of God given to
those who put their faith in Jesus—specifically describing man's
ability to stand before God without guilt or inferiority as if he
had never sinned. But under the old covenant, righteousness
was achieved in a much different manner.

As mentioned in an earlier chapter, Moses told the children
of Israel, "Then it will be righteousness for us, if we are careful
to observe all these commandments before the Lord our God,
as He has commanded us" (Deuteronomy 6:25, NKJV). This
was no easy task because "the person who keeps all of the laws
except one is as guilty as a person who has broken all of God's
laws" (James 2:10). In other words, no matter how well a person
followed the law, righteousness was still God's to give, not his
to earn.

113

Elihu said, "I will fetch my knowledge from afar; I will ascribe righteousness to my Maker." The word "ascribe" means to assign, to credit, or to give attribute to. Elihu understood that righteousness should be assigned and credited to God himself. And it was only God who could assign, credit, or attribute righteousness to us.

Our Choosing

In a fierce challenge against Job and his three friends, Elihu continued setting the record straight about God:

God is mighty, yet he does not despise anyone! He is mighty in both power and understanding... If [people] listen and obey God, they will be blessed with prosperity throughout their lives. All their years will be pleasant. But if they refuse to listen to him, they will cross over the river of death, dying from lack of understanding. For the godless are full of resentment. Even when he punishes them, they refuse to cry out to him for help... Look, God is all-powerful. Who is a teacher like him? No one can tell him what to do. Or say to him, "You have done wrong." Instead, glorify his mighty works, singing songs of praise.

(36:5, 11–13, 22–24)

Elihu was clear about God's might and power, but he was just as clear about God's compassion and understanding. Many tribulations in which we find ourselves are the result of choices we have made. In Deuteronomy 30:19, God said, "Today I have given you the choice between life and death, between blessings and curses. Now I call on heaven and earth to witness the choice you make. Oh, that you would choose life, so that you and your descendants might live!"

God's love and provision for us are constant. They are like an umbrella that never moves. However, when we make choices that move us out from under God's covering, then we are vulnerable to attack. Elihu said, "Do not long for the cover of night, for that is when people will be destroyed" (Job 36:20). Moving away from the light only puts us in darkness. And it is in the dark places that people are swallowed up.

So what is the darkness? Typically it is one of two things. First, it could be ignorance (spiritual blindness or lack of understanding) that gives Satan an opportunity to take advantage of us. When God's people are blinded by ignorance, or by a lack of knowledge, Scripture warns that they may be destroyed (Hosea 4:6; 2 Corinthians 2:11). A second area of darkness is doing anything that puts us outside of God's protection. We find ourselves in such places because of poor choices. In either scenario, however, we are at risk because darkness (of any kind) is Satan's playground.

Devil's Lotto

Whenever we move outside of the realm of God's protection—out from under his umbrella—we move into Satan's territory, whether on purpose or inadvertently. And Satan's arena is dangerous because we become susceptible to what I like to call "Devil's Lotto." God is omniscient, but Satan is not. He isn't God and therefore doesn't know the intents of people's hearts. But if our choices move us out from under God's protection and into Satan's territory, we become fair game for destruction. His weapons are lethal. His aim is good. And Devil's Lotto is simply the luck (or un-luck) of being missed or hit.

But some would argue, "God did this to Job." Did he? According to the first chapter of Job it was Satan who did these things to him. God simply allowed the calamities to occur. But let's understand *why* before we pass judgment. In His righteousness, God could not have permitted all of that destruction had Job not moved out from under His covering. God has given every person a free will to choose. This means knowingly, or sometimes unknowingly, our choices determine our destiny. The point here is that God would not (and could not) have permitted Satan to do anything if Job wasn't already in his hand (Job 2:6).

For centuries, people have come up with all kinds of reasons that sound good in theory as to why Job experienced so much loss. But theories that contradict the *rest* of God's Word and, more specifically, God's character are false. This book is about righting that wrong and helping us all understand so the church as a whole will be strengthened and wiser concerning areas of deception that have kept us weak.

God's Word is truth, and it doesn't contradict itself, even when it seems to. When the Bible says in one place that God destroys and in another place that He protects, then we need to read each scripture in context to get a clear picture. For example, 2 Thessalonians 3:3 says, "But the Lord is faithful, who will establish you and guard you from the evil one" (NKJV). In the context of this scripture, Paul is referring to the righteous, those who are abiding in God. This speaks of His umbrella of protection.

But as already mentioned, God has given every person freewill. Therefore, He won't make us stay under His protection. He only promises that "he who dwells in the secret place of the Most High shall abide under the shadow of the Almighty" (Psalm 91:1, NKJV). David understood this when he fled from Saul into the caves. He said, "Have mercy on me, O God, have mercy! I look to you for protection. I will hide beneath the shadow of your wings until the danger passes by" (Psalm 57:1). David humbled himself and, therefore, positioned himself correctly.

A Compliment?

Another area to note again is God's statement that Job was blameless. We've often put our own definition on this, assuming it described a form of perfection, but notice what the apostle Paul said of himself: "concerning zeal, I persecuted the church;

concerning the righteousness which is in the law, *I was blame-less*" (Philippians 3:6, NKJV, emphasis added). In other words, Paul recognized that as a Pharisee he was able to obey the Jewish law so carefully that he was never accused of any fault.

In the book, *Say Yes!*, Rick Renner made this comment:

> In First Timothy 1:13, Paul described his former self as "a blasphemer, a persecutor, and injurious." The word "blasphemer" means to riducule, to speal ugly, to speak of with no respect. It is particularly used to demonstrate the attitude of a man who has no respect for the things of God. Paul was raised as a strictly religious Jew. But the fact that he would use the word "blasphemer" to describe himself prior to his salvation implies that although his outward service to God was impeccable, his heart was far from God.

So to say Job was blameless is not quite the compliment we may have at first thought. All of us can go through the motions of doing things right. It's even possible to perform the works of God's law so carefully that no one could ever find fault with us. But the real question is (and has always been): What's in our heart?

God was most definitely pleased when His children followed the law as He instructed them to. But when God sent Samuel to the house of Jesse to anoint the next king, whereas Samuel looked at the outward attributes of Jesse's sons, God said, "Don't judge by his appearance or height, for I have rejected him. The Lord doesn't see things the way you see them. People judge by outward appearance, but the Lord looks at the heart" (1 Samuel 16:7). And in Paul's case, *blameless* only described his outward actions—not his heart.

So while Job had emphatically maintained his innocence because he too had carefully obeyed all of his religious duties, it was this mentality that had aroused so much anger in Elihu. Job was clueless that it was the sin of pride and self-righteousness that moved him out from under the full protection of God. If we look again at Job 1:22, we'll find one reason Job was out from under God's umbrella of protection. It states, "Job did not sin by blaming God," which was made in reference to Job's silence *before* his friends arrived. Later on, Job made all kinds of statements that put blame on God—things that must have been buried in the crevices of his heart in order to come out of his mouth.

God doesn't mind us asking for understanding, but Job outright said, "God did this to me" and "God set me up as his target." Job was guilty of blaming God in the midst of trying to understand what was happening to him. Both existed, and one doesn't erase the other. Someone may ask, "Didn't Job blame God simply because of his anguish—after he succumbed to attack?" Yes and no. The adversity simply revealed what was already in his heart. We'll never fully know what, but something in Job's heart had already moved him out from under God's protection. Remember what God said to Satan, "Behold, he is in your hand, but spare his life" (Job 2:6). In other words, "Look. He's already in your hand—just don't kill him."

God couldn't have permitted Satan's attack if Job was still under His shelter. But unintentionally, the sins of Job's heart had moved him away from the full protection of God. To Satan, Job was just another target in the strike zone—operating in the "luck" of never being hit while out on the fringe of Devil's Lotto. This sheds some light on the words of the apostle Peter who warned us, "Be sober, be vigilant, because your adversary the devil walks about like a roaring lion, seeking whom he may devour" (1 Peter 5:8, NKJV). Notice it says, "*whom* he may devour." In other words, the devil is not at liberty to touch just anybody. But know this: he's on the lookout.

Powerful and Merciful

And it seems Elihu understood these things. In fact, it was Job's misconstrued thinking that he'd been wronged that had Elihu so stirred up.

Pay attention to this, Job. Stop and consider the wonderful miracles of God! Do you know how God controls the storm and causes the lightening to flash from his clouds? Do you understand how he moved the clouds with wonderful perfection and skill? When you are sweltering in your clothes and the south wind dies down and everything is still, he makes the skies reflect the heat like a bronze mirror. Can you do that? So teach the rest of us what to say to God. We are too ignorant to make our own arguments. Should God be notified that I want to speak? Can people even speak when they are confused?... We cannot imagine the power of the Almighty, but even though he is just and righteous, he does not destroy us. No wonder people everywhere fear him. All who are wise show him reverence.

(37:14–20, 23–24)

Up until this point, Job had maintained his innocence. Eliphaz, Bildad, and Zophar said it must be Job's sins that brought such calamity upon him, which carry some partial truth because we now understand how Job moved out from under the umbrella of God's protection—even unknowingly. But Job's three friends described God as a tyrant who couldn't wait for His people to make a mistake so He could squash them like bugs—*and this is not correct.*

Elihu is the only one who has a right understanding of God: one who is righteous, just, powerful, patient, *and merciful.*

It's important to get our doctrine right. God's true desire to "crush" something actually has nothing to do with you or me. In a warning to the Romans to avoid divisive people, the apostle Paul revealed who God really wants to crush:

Now I urge you, brethren, note those who cause divisions and offenses, contrary to the doctrine which you learned, and avoid them. For those who are such do not serve our Lord Jesus Christ, but their own belly, and by smooth words and flattering speech deceive the hearts of the simple. For your obedience has become known to all. Therefore I am glad on your behalf; but I want you to be wise in what is good, and simple concerning evil. And the God of peace will *crush Satan* under your feet shortly. The grace of our Lord Jesus Christ be with you. Amen.

' (Romans 16:17–20, NKJV, my italics)

Notice it wasn't the divisive people God wanted to crush, but the one who was behind their rebellion—Satan himself. Our heavenly Father is a God of peace. Satan is behind all destruction. He's the destroyer, not God. So when we're tempted to think that God wants to crush us (as Job and his friends suggest), we need to remember that their emotions got the best of them. Just because they said it doesn't make it true.

And with that, Elihu was finished setting the record straight. He had nothing more to say.

God's Turn

But before anyone could respond, the Lord decided it was time to speak (and confirm Elihu's argument). From a whirlwind, He said to Job,

Who is this that questions my wisdom with such ignorant words? Brace yourself like a man, because I have some questions for you, and you must answer them. Where were you when I laid the foundations of the earth? Tell me, if you know so much... Have you ever commanded the morning to appear and caused the dawn to rise in the east?... Where does the light come from, and where does the darkness go? Can you take each to its home? Do you know how to get there? But of course you know all this! For you were born before it was all created, and you are so very experienced!... Do you still want to argue with the Almighty? You are God's critic, but do you have the answers?

(38:2–4, 12, 19-21; 40:2)

It seems God had had enough of all their foolish talk. If God were as hard as Job's three friends thought, He would have interrupted with a lightning bolt and responded long before now. But instead He has patiently listened and now wants to hush them up. I'm sure this encounter with Almighty God had them all shaking in their boots. But more than that, I believe their hearts and minds had been fully awakened by God's awesome presence. Whatever they so fervently believed before has now became futile. They, like Nebuchadnezzar, have had their spiritual sanity returned to them.

"Then Job replied to the LORD, 'I am nothing—how could I ever find the answers? I will cover my mouth with my hand. I have said too much already. I have nothing more to say'" (40:3–5). Job made a good decision. Amos 5:13 says, "Those who are wise will keep quiet." And Zephaniah 1:7 instructs the wise to "be silent in the presence of the Lord GOD" (NKJV).

CHAPTER TEN

Read Job, Chapters 40-42

The Lord Speaks

Light has been shed on the darkness of Job's heart. Simple revelation is usually all that's needed to convict. And words often are inadequate at moments of true understanding. Many of us walk through our homes at night without turning on any lights because we think we know where everything is, but occasionally we stub a toe. When the lights are turned on, we can see what was in our way. In the same way, God is light, and in His presence all things are revealed. I don't believe Job was simply consenting to God because he was afraid of Him. I believe the magnificent light of God's presence humbled Job and revealed the dark areas of self-righteousness that unintentionally crept into his heart.

The Opposite of Pride

But God wasn't through reprimanding him.

Then the LORD answered Job from the whirlwind: "Brace yourself like a man, because I have some questions for you, and you must answer them. Will you discredit my justice and condemn me just to prove you are right? Are you as strong as God? Can you thunder with a voice like his? All right, put on your glory and splendor, your honor and majesty. Give vent to your anger. Let it overflow against the proud. Humiliate the proud with a glance; walk on the wicked where they stand. Bury them in the dust. Imprison them in the world of the dead. Then even I would praise you, for your own strength would save you."

(40:6–14)

It seems so silly now that God had to remind Job that he had no ability whatsoever to save himself. But how many times have we done the same thing? How many times have we had an attitude of self-righteousness as well?

Then Job replied to the LORD: "I know that you can do anything, and no one can stop you. You ask, 'Who is this that questions my wisdom with such ignorance?' It is I—and I was talking about things I knew nothing about, things far too wonderful for me. You said, 'Listen and I will speak! I have some questions for you, and you must answer them.' I had only heard about you before, but now I have seen you with my own eyes. I take back everything

I said, and I sit in dust and ashes to show my repentance.

(42:1–6)

God's mercy and patience have finally retrieved for Him what He was looking for. Psalm 51:17 says, "My [only] sacrifice [acceptable] to God is a broken spirit; a broken and contrite heart [broken with sorrow for sin, thoroughly penitent], such, O God, You will not despise" (AMP). God wants us to have understanding, and when understanding comes, He wants us to repent. Repentance is the opposite of pride because true repentance reveals *humility*, often bringing us to our knees in gratitude before God.

Have You Not Known Me?

Job's repentance was interesting in that he said, "I had heard about you before, but now I have seen you with my own eyes." In so many ways, this statement sums up the reason Job was unknowingly blinded by pride and self-righteousness. Although God knew him, he did not know God.

It's sad to think we can be raised in church our entire lives and still never know Him. And yet it's possible—Jesus himself had to ask one of his closest disciples, "Have I been with you so long, and yet you have not known Me, Philip?" (John 14:9, NKJV) The disciples spent three years of their lives, night and day, with Jesus. Yet in spite of that, they too didn't really know Him. Sometimes our training to know right and wrong becomes so traditionalized, passed down from generation to generation, that we end up only knowing the law and not the Maker of the law.

I became a Christian as an adult, so I am well aware of what God has saved me from. And for this reason, I strive to remain grateful for all He has done for me. I greatly desire for my own children to know Him this way also. I wasn't raised in church, but my children don't know life without it. It would be so easy for them to merely "hear" about God, but I want them, like Job, to say, "I have seen you with my own eyes."

A Show of Mercy

This was God's intention all along—for Job and his friends to see Him and know Him. Job's eyes had been opened, and its was now time for Eliphaz, Bildad, and Zophar to see God too.

> After the LORD had finished speaking to Job, He said to Eliphaz the Temanite: "I am angry with you and with your two friends, for you have not spoken accurately about me, as my servant Job has. So take seven young bulls and seven rams and go to my servant Job and offer a burnt offering for yourselves. My servant Job will pray for you, and I will accept his prayer on your behalf. I will not treat you as you deserve, for you have not spoken accurately about me, as my servant Job has."
>
> (Job 42:7-8)

God's statement here has baffled many people because it almost sounds as if Job was right in everything he said about God, but let's not lose sight of the context. The New King James Version says, "...the Lord said to Eliphaz the Temanite, 'My wrath is aroused against you and your two friends, for you have not spoken of Me what is right, as My servant Job has'" (verse 7). Two things to note here is that God clearly points out Eliphaz and his two friends—not his three friends. This is helpful lest we think Elihu is being corrected with the group. On the contrary, Elihu spoke correctly of God and His righteousness.

The second (and maybe most important) thing to note is what God meant when He said Job spoke what was right, but Eliphaz and his friends did not.

We just saw God show up in a big way to correct how wrong Job had been about Him, so this statement that Job spoke "what was right" is not a reference to his rantings in previous chapters. God is specifically speaking of Job's repentance. Listen again to *what Job said right*:

I know that You can do everything, and that no purpose of Yours can be withheld from You. You asked, "Who is this who hides counsel without knowledge?" Therefore I uttered what I did not understand, things too wonderful for me, which I did not know. Listen, please, and let me speak; You said, "I will question you, and you shall answer Me." I have heard of You by the hearing of the ear, but now my eye sees You. Therefore I abhor myself, and repent in dust and ashes.

(Job 42:2-6, NKJV, my emphasis)

In David's prayer of repentance after acknowledging his sin with Bathsheba, he said, "The sacrifices of God are a broken spirit, a broken and a contrite heart—these, O God, you will not despise" (Psalm 51:17, NKJV). The Bible says when we repent God removes our transgressions as far as the east is from the west. There's no record of Job's friends repenting for their slanderous statements about God (like Job did). Therefore, in their lack of repentance, they didn't say what was "right" as Job did. In other words, God may have corrected Job's self-righteous behavior, but He also readily accepted his remorse.

First John 1:9 says, "If we confess our sins, He is faithful and just to forgive us our sins and cleanse us of all unrighteousness" (NKJV). Job said some hard things about God, but when it was brought into the light, Job was truly remorseful. He was guilty of self-righteousness and talking foolishly from his flesh, but Eliphaz, Bildad, and Zophar were guilty of blaspheming God's character with little or no remorse. To blaspheme means to speak evil of deity[5], and later, under the law of Moses, this was a sin punishable by death.

Leviticus 24:15–16 states, "Those who curse their God will be punished for their sin. Anyone who blasphemes the Name of the Lord must be stoned to death by the whole community of Israel. Any native-born Israelite or foreigner among you who blasphemes the Name of the Lord must be put to death." Job's friends were guilty of blaspheming God's character of love and mercy, and therefore, should pay the consequence. But until that moment, Eliphaz and his friends hadn't even realized they were guilty of blaspheming God. All the things they said of

Him, they honestly believed to be true. But now, the light of God's presence has opened their eyes as well. They were wrong about God. He is loving and merciful. He doesn't desire that any person perish. And this revelation is about to be proven to them.

To demonstrate His mercy and show them how wrong they are about Him, instead of a harsh punishment or death, God requires only a sacrifice and a prayer for their sins. I'd like to think they never forgot the kindness God showed them. When a person has a shallow understanding of their sin, they will also have a shallow understanding of God's mercy. But when a person has a great understanding of God's mercy, they will also have a loud voice of praise. Hopefully Eliphaz, Bildad, and Zophar spent the rest of their days testifying of God's great compassion and leniency. Like the psalmist, they may have declared, "Come and listen, all you who fear God, and I will tell you what he did for me" (Psalm 66:16).

Glory Revealed

God's Word, and His commandments, was established to help guide His people until the Messiah came. But through the course of time, Satan deceived people into believing God was hard and unrelenting. The righteousness that came from obeying the law gave people a measure of being made right with God, but Satan couldn't stand it. He had been cast from God's presence, and it became his goal to separate as many people from God as possible. By making them believe God is a tyrant waiting for their downfall, or by puffing them up with pride, Satan succeeds. And although Satan is the god of this world, God is still *God Almighty*. And the truth of who the Lord is will be revealed as the Scriptures promise: "The glory of the LORD shall be revealed, and all flesh shall see it together; for the mouth of the LORD has spoken" (Isaiah 40:5 NKJV).

The glory that shall be revealed is that God is good and His mercy endures forever:

"Oh, give thanks to the LORD, for He is good! For His mercy endures forever" (1 Chronicles 16:34 NKJV). "Praise the LORD! Oh, give thanks to the LORD, for He is good! For His mercy endures forever" (Psalm 106:1 NKJV).

Eliphaz, Bildad, and Zophar experienced God's mercy firsthand. And Job found restoration. "When Job prayed for his friends, the LORD restored his fortunes. In fact, the LORD gave him twice as much as before! Job lived 140 years after that, living to see four generations of his children and grandchildren. Then he died, an old man who had lived a long, good life" (42:10, 16–17).

Job's restoration is directly related to God's mercy and God's glory. His later years have never been forgotten, and it has encouraged many generations to trust God, no matter how things may seem at the moment.

God's Ultimate Intent

So, it was never God's intention for Job to be utterly destroyed. In the book of James, we find God's purpose concerning Job:

My brethren, take the prophets, who spoke in the name of the Lord, as an example of suffering and patience. Indeed we count them blessed who endure. You have heard of the perseverance of Job and seen the end intended by the Lord—that the Lord is very compassionate and merciful.

(James 5:10–11, NKJV)

God loved Job very much, as He does all of His children. And every loving father corrects his children when they stray. "My son, do not despise the chastening of the LORD, nor detest His correction; For whom the LORD loves He corrects, just as a father the son in whom he delights" (Proverbs 3:11–12, NKJV). Sometimes it is through correction that we learn just how much we are really loved.

God's intent was to show His mercy. And in the end, the error in Job's heart was revealed and he and his friends were brought to a new place of understanding. God would now be glorified through them. There is no doubt Eliphaz, Bildad, and Zophar would testify of God's goodness every time they spoke of the mercy they received from Him. And Job, too, would be sure to give glory to God by passing down from generation to generation the truth about Him and His righteousness.

The book of Job has unquestionably been the subject of much curiosity and discussion. It is even regarded by many as the oldest book in the Bible, while others place it as late as the exile. But either way, it shows us God desires greatly for all men to understand who He truly is—while also understanding the schemes of Satan. Of course, the devil has found many ways of blaspheming God's character, including distorting man's interpretation of the book of Job. It has been a source of great controversy for a long time—especially among believers. It is unfortunate however, that so many people still teach to this day that every bad thing that happens is God's doing. And it's even more unfortunate some of them use the book of Job to try to prove it.

Adversities in life can teach us valuable lessons. And, yes, God may allow us to walk through hard times to strengthen us. This does not mean, however, that He's the one who sends every calamity or that He turns His head, as if He doesn't care when we hurt. "Even when I walk through the darkest valley, I will not be afraid, for you are close beside me. Your rod and your staff protect and comfort me" (Psalm 23:4). Even the psalmist understood God is with us in the storm. He's not the cause of the storm.

But there is an adversary, and God wants us to learn how to endure and overcome, because "the devil is poised to pounce, and would like nothing better than to catch you napping" (1 Peter 5:8, MSG).

CHAPTER ELEVEN

Is God in Control of Everything?

Satan's tricks haven't changed. He revealed himself as a deceiver in the Garden of Eden, and he has continued deceiving mankind ever since. The Bible calls him the father of lies. His goal has always been to separate people from God, just as he was separated.

The Big If

As we've seen through Job's life, God is not in control of everything. Our own opinions, choices, and beliefs make and create scenarios and situations God is not involved with. But when a tragedy has happened or some event is unexplainable, people often say things like, "Well, you know God has a reason. He's in control of everything that happens."

Is He? If God is in control of everything, why would we need to pray at all?

Just consider this: Is there crime in heaven? Is there tragedy in heaven? Sickness? Death? Evil? Obviously not. These things do not exist in heaven, which is why Jesus said, "In this manner, therefore, pray: Our Father *in heaven*, hallowed be Your name. Your kingdom come. Your will be done *on earth* as it is in heaven" (Matthew 6:9–10, NKJV, emphasis added).

Think about what Jesus said. He told us to pray for things on earth to reflect how things are in heaven. But if God is in control of everything already, then why would He need us to pray for this?

Psalm 115:16 says, "The heaven, even the heavens, are the Lord's; but the earth He has given to the children of men" (NKJV). This explains a lot. Heaven is a place of great peace, and free of offenses of any kind, because it belongs to the Lord. He's in control there. But the earth is a mess—a dangerous place, really—because humans have been put in charge of it.

So is God in control of everything? No, He really isn't.

For example, God didn't have control over what you did yesterday. You chose what you would wear, what you ate, what you said, where you went, and the attitude you carried all day. And these are just minor examples of decisions made my mankind every day. My point is that we need to understand that in His power and wisdom, God saw fit to let you and I choose a lot of things—but not without direction:

> Now it shall come to pass, if you diligently obey the voice of the Lord your God, to observe carefully all His commandments which I command you today, that the Lord your God will set you high above all nations of the earth. And all these blessings shall

come upon you and overtake you, because you obey the voice of the Lord your God. But it shall come to pass if you do not obey the voice of the Lord your God, to observe carefully all His commandments and His statues which I command you today, that all these curses will come upon you and overtake you.

(Deuteronomy 28:1–2, 15, NKJV)

God put a big *if* in our world.

He said *if* we carefully observe, obey, and choose His ways, then we will be blessed. But *if* we ignore and do not obey the counsel of His word, then tragedy may befall us. God is a good Father, and He has given us, His children, the opportunity to experience His goodness—*if* we will choose wisely.

The word *if* indicates choice. God is not in control of everything, and believers who love their good Father should defend His name when people accuse Him of causing some tragedy that was obviously the result of men who forged their own path and left God behind.

"I call heaven and earth as witnesses today against you, that I have set before you life and death, blessing and cursing; therefore choose life, that both you and your descendants may live" (Deuteronomy 30:19, NKJV). Let me say it this way: *if* God were in control of everything, there would be no choice, and there would be no *if.*

Jesus himself helped substantiate this in His teachings. For example, in the parable of the wedding, He said:

The kingdom of heaven is like a certain king who arranged a marriage for his son, and sent out his servants to call those who were invited to the wedding; and they were not willing to come. Again, he sent out other servants, saying, "Tell those who are invited, 'See, I have prepared my dinner; my oxen and fatted cattle are killed, and all things are ready. Come to the wedding.'" But they made light of it and went their ways, one to his own farm, another to his business. And the rest seized his servants, treated them spitefully, and killed them.

(Matthew 22:1–6, NKJV)

Those who were invited had a choice. Jesus said they "were not willing to come." In fact, Jesus said the people made light of the invitation and went their own way. Does this sound at all like people today? I think so. In other words, not everything is the *will* of God. He has given us a free will.

So even with good intentions, we often make light of God's instructions for our lives depending on how we feel at the moment. But if we're not careful, these subjective choices can give our enemy admittance to areas of our lives he should not be able to access. As the apostle Paul said, "We don't want to give Satan an opening for yet more mischief" (2 Corinthians 2:11, MSG).

Here's another parable that illustrates our ability to choose. Jesus said, "What do you think? A man had two sons, and he came to the first and said, 'Son, go, work today in my vineyard.' He answered and said, 'I will not,' but afterward he regretted it and went. Then he came to the second and said likewise. And he answered and said, 'I go, sir,' but he did not go. Which of the two did the will of his father? They said to Him, 'The first'" (Matthew 21:28–31, NKJV).

This again illustrates God's design to let people choose. He is not in control of everything.

Why, Lord?

Recently I was praying while the TV was on, and I saw a short segment on some workhouses in India where young boys were acid-washing designer jeans for the United States. They were working in horrible conditions, and the faces of these young people revealed their fatigue and emptiness.

In my spirit, I said, "Why, Lord?" And very quickly, I heard this reply in my spirit, "They live in a godless country." Without further explanation, I understood what God meant. How can we expect the world to be a good place when, in many parts of it, God is not invited, much less recognized? By itself, the earth is not a good place. But isn't this why Jesus came, to restore the broken relationship between God and man in a broken and subjected world?

Everything is a big word. It describes the total of all things. Yet when we look at our world and compare what we see with Scripture and with our understanding of our good God, obvious contradictions appear. God can't possibly be in control of everything. So why do so many say that He is?

I heard one minister call this: "No-Fault Religion"—and I agree. When someone can't explain something, they pull a theological rabbit out of their hat and say, "Well, God must have had a reason." Really? God has a reason for a young child dying of cancer, or a teenager being killed in a car accident? God has a reason for a father losing his job, or a mother being taken from her children?

There is a reason, all right, but it's not because God is doing it, for that would contradict His own Word.

We have known and believed the love that God has for us. God is love, and he who abides in love abides in God, and God in him. Love has been perfected among us in this: that we may have boldness in the day of judgment; because as He is, so are we in this world. There is no fear in love, but perfect love casts out fear, because fear involves torment. But he who fears has not been made perfect in love.

(1 John 4:16–18, NKJV)

We could say it this way: He who fears has a lack of understanding of God's love and His care for us.

So let's be perfectly clear: God loves us! He doesn't need to send tragedy upon us to teach us a lesson or to accomplish His will. God will, however, allow us to walk through things to learn a lesson (like the example I gave of my son keeping his room clean or not), but He's not the one doing the killing, stealing, and destroying in our world—that is going on because we have an enemy.

"We know that all things work together for good to those who love God, to those who are called according to His purpose" (Romans 8:28, NKJV). Many people only quote the first half of this verse, but notice that God is able to help (and intervene) for those *who love him*—not just in word, but in faith, sincerity, and action.

Know Your Enemy

It is important for us to resist Satan and strengthen our relationship with God. This is one of the main messages Jesus emphasized during His life and ministry. Have you ever considered how little the Bible speaks of Satan in the Old Testament? There's references in Genesis at the fall of man and prophecies in Isaiah of Lucifer's ejection from heaven, but not much more beyond that. But Jesus wasn't shy about exposing Satan at all.

In Matthew, he explained how the devil was the one who sowed the tares (13:39). In Luke, Jesus revealed how Satan comes to take the Word out of people's hearts, lest they should believe and be saved (8:12). He called out those who didn't believe the truth as followers of their "father the devil" (John 8:44). In the book of Acts, Peter explained "how God anointed Jesus of Nazareth with the Holy Spirit and with power, who went about doing good and healing all who were oppressed by the devil, for God was with Him" (10:38, NKJV). And John added: "For this purpose the Son of God was manifested, that He might destroy the works of the devil" (1 John 3:8, NKJV).

Jesus defended His Father by exposing the tactics and strategies of the enemy. And then the ultimate victory was accomplished at the death, burial, and resurrection of Christ— when Jesus retrieved the authority Satan took in the Garden and gave it back to God's children.

But even after becoming followers of Christ, we still have a choice to follow God *partially* or *fully*; adhering to all of His word, or only to the parts we like. Satan knows we carry the authority and that we have a choice, which is why he works through deception and ignorance. He wants nothing more than to ruin God's good name.

His Mercy Endures Forever

The lesson God intended for us to learn through the book of Job has less to do with Job and more to do with revealing deception and proving God's compassion and mercy.

Let us not be deceived: the devil is mad, and he'd like nothing better than to take everyone down with him. This is why he jumped at the chance to hurt Job. God knew how Job's story would end: He would be glorified through Job's life. His true character of love and mercy (which Satan tried to ruin) would be made known to every succeeding generation, and Satan would be exposed as the destroyer.

So how is it that religion has twisted this truth into naming God as the ransacker of people's lives? Remember, antonyms for the word *destroyer* are author, creator, restorer—the names of our God. He is anything but a destroyer.

The end intended by the Lord, as seen through the perseverance of Job, is that God is very compassionate and merciful.

Everything the devil has ever done had only one intent, and that was to keep people from walking in the light of God's love. But Jesus destroyed the works of the devil

By taking upon Himself the sins of the world, we no longer have to perform a certain set of commandments to earn God's approval. We simply have to believe in the One who paid our debt. Second Corinthians 5:21 sums up God's ultimate intent: to make Jesus, who was innocent and without sin, to be sin for us who were and are guilty of all kinds of sin. He did this so we could be assured that we were right with God and had the ability to stand before him without any guilt or inferiority, as if we had never sinned.

This is *true* righteousness versus self-righteousness. One is of humbleness, faith, and mercy, and the other is not.

Faith is the Difference

In Romans 10:4, we are told, "Christ is the end of the law for righteousness to everyone who believes" (NKJV). This means our faith in Jesus puts an end to our need to earn righteousness through the things we do. Righteousness describes our right-standing with God, including a guilt-free relationship with Him.

However, without a little help in this area, people are often stubborn concerning this subject. "For they don't understand God's way of making people right with himself. Refusing to accept God's way, they cling to their own way of getting right with God by trying to keep the law" (Romans 10:3). This is what Job did.

But faith is the difference between God's righteousness and the rightness the law offered under the Old Covenant. "For Moses writes that the law's way of making a person right with God requires obedience to all of its commands" (Romans 10:5). In other words, trying to do things in our own merit to get God's approval is the exact opposite of what God desires.

Earning our righteousness by obeying all of God's commands was the approach of the old covenant. We now have a new and better covenant with Jesus Christ. Paul tell us that God made Jesus "who knew no sin to be sin for us, that we might become the righteousness of God in Him" (2 Corinthians 5:21, NKJV). So our standing with God is no longer based on works, but on faith.

So let's be clear. Under the new covenant, the need to *earn* our right-standing with God has been abolished. This is a hard truth to grasp. But even Jesus clarified what is required to please God: "Then they said to Him, 'What shall we do, that we may work the works of God?' Jesus answered and said to them, 'This is the work of God, that you *believe* in Him whom He sent'" (John 6:28–29, emphasis added). The church as a whole understands this statement, but the devil has twisted it, causing people to subconsciously believe the only way to gain God's approval is through outward actions (regardless of inward misgivings).

His Loving Kindness

God didn't punish Job, Eliphaz, Bildad, or Zophar in former times, and He isn't looking to punish you or me either. He is kind and merciful, and He "saved us and called us with a holy calling, not according to our works, but according to His own purpose and grace which was given to us in Christ Jesus before time began" (2 Timothy 1:9 NKJV). We can't claim our righteousness as something we have earned. On our own, we are never innocent.

> But when God our Savior revealed his kindness and love, he saved us, not because of the righteous things we had done, but because of his mercy. He washed away our sins, giving us a new birth and a new life through the Holy Spirit. He generously poured out the Spirit upon us through Jesus Christ our Savior. Because of his grace he made us right in his sight and gave us confidence that we will inherit eternal life.
>
> (Titus 3:4–7)

Martin Luther once said, "I have held many things in my hands and lost them all. But whatever I've placed in God's hands, that I still possess." Sometimes only a few words are needed to express a great truth. In our lives, dreams and hopes have come and gone, but the ones we truly gave to God are never lost. They are continually held in His strength, in His timing, and in His perfect love.

I can't tell you how many times I have been troubled by fleeting questions such as, "Am I still in the will of God?" Or "Did I miss you, Father?" When I look only on the natural side, I can sometimes forget for a moment that God's plans never fail. In such moments the words of Paul are both comforting and promising:

> But what things were gain to me, these I have counted loss for Christ. Yet indeed I also count all things loss for the excellence of the knowledge of Christ Jesus my Lord, for whom I have suffered the loss of all things, and count them as rubbish, that I may gain Christ and be found in Him, not having my own righteousness, which is from the law, but that which is through faith in Christ, the righteousness which is from God by faith; that I may know Him and the power of His resurrection.
> (Philippians 3:7–10, NKJV)

His words are comforting, because we are reminded that loss does not have to be a negative. His words hold promise, because God always replaces what we give Him with something better.

And if there is anything I know for sure, it is that God is faithful.

Paul told Timothy, "If we are faithless, He remains faithful. He cannot deny Himself" (2 Timothy 2:13, NKJV). We must believe this—and live by it. You and I will fail at times, but God never will.

In closing, I want to quote Charles Spurgeon from his writings in *All of Grace*. As we remember Job, I pray this will be our renewed mindset:

> Beware of mixing even a little of self with the mortar with which you build, or you will make it untempered mortar, and the stones will not hold together. If you look to Christ for your beginnings, beware of looking to yourself for your endings. He is Alpha. See to it that you make Him Omega also. If you begin in the Spirit you must not hope to be made perfect by the flesh. Begin as you mean to go on, and go on as you began, and let the Lord be all in all in you.[6]

Notes

Chapter One

[1]Thompson, Frank Charles. Thompson Chain-Reference Study Bible (B. B. Kirkbride Bible Company, Inc., 1997), 1781.

Chapter Two

[2]The Complete Word Study Dictionary: Old Testament (AMG Publishers, 1994).

Chapter Three

[3]The Complete Word Study Dictionary: Old Testament (AMG Publishers, 1994).

Chapter Seven

[4]Easton's 1897 Bible Dictionary (Database: NavPress Software, 1996).

Chapter Ten

[5]Thompson Chain-Reference Study Bible, 1687.

Chapter Eleven

[6]Spurgeon, Charles. <u>All of Grace</u> (Database: NavPress Software, 1997), excerpt from the chapter entitled, "The Fear of Final Falling."

About the Author

Daphne Delay has been writing and speaking since 1999, when she was first asked to share at a women's conference. She didn't know at the time how profound that first speaking engagement would be. But God knew…

Daphne now travels and speaks frequently. She is the wife of a senior pastor and works side-by-side with her husband in the ministry at Family Harvest Church in Seminole, Texas. She is actively involved in their women's ministry and enjoys helping new believers build a foundation for a victorious life.

Daphne is an active sports mom who loves attending all her kids' events. Besides writing, her favorite hobby is delving into anything having to do with new technology. She doesn't mind being the nerd friend, but what she wants to be remembered for most is: Spreading the good news of His righteousness!

Contact Daphne

Daphne speaks frequently on the topic of righteousness. She can share a keynote, half-day, full-day, or retreat version of this content, depending on your needs. For more information, please visit her website at *daphnedelay.com*.

You can also connect with Daphne here:

Twitter: *twitter.com/daphnedelay*
Facebook: *facebook.com/daphnedelay*

For group or individual study, please check out the **companion workbook for** *Facing the Mirror,* which can be found at daphnedelay.com.

PRAYER OF SALVATION

God loves you—no matter who you are, no matter what your past. God loves you so much that he gave his one and only begotten Son for you. The Bible tells us that "... whoever believes in him shall not perish but have eternal life" (John 3:16 NIV). Jesus laid down His life and rose again so that we could spend eternity with Him and experience His absolute best on earth. If you would like to receive Jesus into your life, say the following prayer out loud and mean it in your heart.

Heavenly Father, I come to you admitting that I am a sinner. Right now, I choose to turn away from sin, and I ask you to cleanse me of all unrighteousness. I believe that Your son, Jesus, died on the cross to take away my sins. I also believe that he rose again from the dead so that I might be forgiven of my sins and made righteous through faith in him. I call upon the name of Jesus Christ to be the Savior and Lord of my life. Jesus, I choose to follow You and ask You that You fill me with the power of the Holy Spirit. I declare that right now I am a child of God. I am free from sin and full of the righteousness of God. I am saved in Jesus' name. Amen.

If you prayed this prayer to receive Jesus Christ as your Savior for the first time, please contact us to receive a free book by writing to us.

www.harrisonhouse.com
Harrison House
PO Box 35035
Tulsa, Oklahoma 74153

The Harrison House Vision

Proclaiming the truth and the power

Of the Gospel of Jesus Christ

With excellence;

Challenging Christians to

Live victoriously,

Grow spiritually,

Know God intimately.

Fast. Easy.
Convenient.

For the latest Harrison House product information and author news, look no further than your computer. All the details on our powerful, life-changing products are just a click away. New releases, E-mail subscriptions, testimonies, monthly specials—find it all in one place. Visit harrisonhouse.com today!

harrisonhouse